Adam's Deep Sleep

The Passion of Jesus Christ Prefigured in the Old Testament

BY FR JAMES MAWDSLEY

NEW OLD

Cover: Diego Velásquez (1599 - 1660) *Christ Crucified*

Scripture quotes are from Sacred Bible: Catholic Public Domain Version unless noted as RSVCE (Catholic Edition of the Revised Standard Version, copyright © 1965, 1966 National Council of Churches USA. Used by permission. All rights reserved worldwide); or DRB (Douay-Rheims Bible, in the public domain); or else as noted in place. Apologies for any omissions or errors in attributing quotes or gaining necessary permissions. Corrections may be made to future editions.

Published by New Old
© 2022 Fr James Mawdsley
ISBN 978-1-7395816-0-2

*I stand unto this day, witnessing both
to small and great, saying no other thing than those
which the prophets and Moses did say should come to pass:
That Christ should suffer, and that He should be the first
that should rise from the dead, and should shew light
to the people, and to the Gentiles.*

— Acts 26:22-23 (DRB)

FOR MY FATHER

Contents

THE PASSION OF JESUS CHRIST PREFIGURED IN THE OLD TESTAMENT

The Passion of Jesus Christ stands at the centre of history. The Crucifixion of the Son of God has directed billions of souls through the centuries subsequent to it, and amazingly gives the greatest light and meaning to all human lives in the centuries prior to it. In the Old Testament (OT) we discover how Jesus' death on the Cross was anticipated even from the first generations. Evidently, Jesus' Sacrifice on Calvary was part of God's plan from the beginning. If we understand what was written about Christ's Sacrifice long before it happened, we have a better chance of understanding what it means for us today.

Whoever loves Jesus Christ never grows tired of learning about Him. Finding Our Saviour's Sacrifice concealed in the Scriptures centuries before it happened corroborates our faith, so that it becomes invincible, as the evidence accumulates that this can only be God's work. We receive profound comfort in our present trials by meditating on the OT saints and seeing how the Cross transformed the meaning of their lives. Of course studying the Passion of Christ in the OT is only possible in light of the New Testament (NT). Ultimately this approach serves the salvation of souls.

To this end, this book examines sixteen OT stories involving mystical sleeps, each of which points to the Crucifixion of Christ. In combination, these stories highlight numerous goods of the Cross: as the true Tree of Life; as the place we discover our Mother; as our battle standard for the total victory of good over evil; and we discern that the Cross divides the right from the left, the Good Thief from the Bad, the sheep from the goats, Heaven from hell.

Next we revisit five biblical accounts which illustrate what was contained in the Blood and water which flowed from Jesus' side, pierced on the Cross. As Jesus' Sacred Heart is central to His Crucifixion, and vital matter for our contemplation, these five enigmatic episodes help us search into His unsearchable Heart. As with the sixteen mystical sleeps, finding Christ our Beloved where we did not expect to find Him elates us. To learn from the Scriptures what comes from His Sacred Heart is to know what He holds dear, what He loves, His inner life. The Bible gives us answers, simple and profound: the Church, the Saints, the Sacraments, Wisdom, Grace.

How can it be that such details were written down centuries before the event? How can it be that millions study the Scriptures without seeing any of this? The OT is notoriously obscure, difficult to understand. The Cross itself is also a great mystery.

But they clarify each other. Combining them does not increase the difficulty, rather the Cross unlocks the OT, revealing the goal to which it all points. And the OT describes attributes of the Cross, giving numerous indications of what Jesus' Death and Resurrection achieves. So we return to the NT with a fuller discernment. There is an interaction: the Paschal Mystery of the NT illuminates the whole of history, including the OT and our own experience. Understanding all this better gives us greater insight into the Passion of Christ itself, raising it even higher in our estimation, attaching us to Jesus more devotedly.

This will be easier to understand through the examples treated in detail in this book. Here I will mention only a few. When we first read that God sent a deep sleep upon Adam, we might think no more of it. When we read Noah lay in a drunken stupor, we are not sure of its relevance. When we hear a great and dread dark fell upon Abraham, we might mistakenly think it begins and ends with him. But once we believe the Cross is the centre of history, informing one way or another every human life, then the strange sleeps of Adam, Noah and Abraham can be decoded.

Adam shows that from the Crucifixion comes Christ's Bride the Church. Noah shows that what hangs on the Cross is Judgement. Abraham shows that Christ's Sacrifice cuts a New and Eternal Covenant. Though we already believed these aspects of Christ's crucifixion, our faith is strengthened to find it depicted so long in advance. That these great men point to Christ raises our esteem for the Cross even higher. Though we believed already Jesus is the Son of God, we see more closely how He was at work from the beginning. We are now better disposed to recognise the Crucifixion prefigured in the outstretched arms of Moses as the Israelites defeated the Amalekites, or the outstretched arms of

Samson as he brought down the godless temple. Once again, our estimation of the Cross is raised higher as we become more convinced by these examples that it means the victory of good over evil.

Gradually we become willing, even hungry, to search for Calvary and its essential elements in the OT. As the Mother of God's presence under the Cross was crucial, we may legitimately search for allusions to Mary as Co-Redemptrix in the OT. And if we search, we are not disappointed. The Virgin Mary's engagement on Calvary is anticipated in Rebekah's first encounter with Isaac and in Ruth adoring at the feet of Boaz.

The Cross makes sense of all these OT stories, and they in turn show the power and meaning of the Cross. This resonance of saving truth which reverberates between the two Testaments, and with our own lives, increases our awe at Christ and also our regard for the OT saints. We glimpse here on earth aspects of the glory which they now enjoy in fullness up in Heaven.

God does not want us to consult the NT alone to understand His gifts and mysteries. He also wants us to read the OT, to understand what His saints went through and why, and to love them. The OT saints are His saints. We want to be with them in Heaven, therefore it is best to start becoming acquainted with them now. They in turn will show us the way to Heaven, which is Jesus Christ.

CORROBORATION OF OUR FAITH

Recognising prefigurations of Jesus Christ in the OT greatly strengthens our faith. Not only does God's power inspire awe, so too does the scope of His reach and His attention to detail. Repeated reading of the OT reveals the Son of God touching ever more lives. He surprises us because maybe we read a passage dozens of times before discovering Him there. He can also use any circumstances to serve His saving purpose, regardless of whether an action is holy, good, bad, strange, wicked or otherwise unintelligible. Convinced by our study that He truly governs everything, down to the merest detail, we can easily trust Him entirely with our lives, too.

In His plan for salvation, God will not allow that His Good News to us be corrupted or lost. He ensures, with man's cooperation, that the Gospel of Jesus Christ is securely transmitted through the centuries by Sacred Scripture and Tradition.[1] Both teach Christ was crucified for the redemption of the world. This is plain in the NT and it is the very meaning of Holy Mass, our chief tradition. Yet this teaching is subject to countless secular and religious attacks. One defence against them is delving ever deeper into the OT. There we discover constantly reiterated that which was ordained from before the foundation of the world: our Salvation through the Passion of Christ. This being God's Plan is communicated by the Bible in so many ways that, for those whose hearts are open to the message, no room is left for doubt.

Certain prefigurations and prophecies of the Passion are clear. For example, St Paul interprets the Passover Lamb as a figure for

---

[1] Council of Trent, *Session IV*, 1.

the Crucified Christ (1 Cor 5:7). The scapegoat, too, foreshadows Jesus, Who is the most famous scapegoat of all. The Suffering Servant of Isaiah 50-53 is so close a description of Christ's Passion that St Jerome, St Augustine and St Isidore classed it as a 'Fifth Gospel' written in advance. Psalm 21 and Wisdom 2 could be put in the same category. Job in his patient and prayerful suffering is a striking type of Jesus. Zechariah prophesies a detail of Calvary so significant that St John pointedly emphasises it in His Gospel: *"They shall look upon him, whom they have pierced"* (Jn 19:37; Zech 12:10).

Besides these, the OT contains numerous, less obvious references to the Crucifixion. It takes more work to discover them, more thought to recognise them. The stories examined below are unique, intriguing, profound, and suggestive of something universal. Yet what? Each story seems incomplete. It is not that they require an ending (real life does not have endings — not yet), but they beg to be decoded or unlocked. Why were they even written? Jesus Christ is the key, the perfect key, the only key to make sense of them all. Through Him alone, what lies hidden becomes revealed.

Jesus taught His Apostles the meaning of the OT, saying after His Resurrection:

> *'all things must be fulfilled which are written in the law of Moses, and in the Prophets, and in the Psalms about Me.'*
> *Then He opened their mind, so that they might understand the Scriptures.* (Lk 24:44-45)

"Moses", *"the Prophets"* and *"the Psalms"* mean the Torah (Law), the Neviim (Prophets) and the Ketuvim (Writings), which

6

as an acronym spell the Tanakh, that is, the entire Hebrew Bible. Jesus is there throughout!

Jesus taught this Scriptural understanding to His Apostles; they passed it on to the Church Fathers, who show how Jesus is to be found on, it seems, every page of the OT. Outstandingly productive were St Irenæus of Lyon explaining the opening chapters of Genesis, St Justin Martyr on the whole Torah, St Gregory Nazianzus on the Prophets, St Bede on Tobit and the Tabernacle, Origen on everything. Without the Fathers, we can scarcely penetrate the surface of the page.

Three of the most inspiring Fathers — St Augustine, St Jerome and St Ephraim — make intriguing connections between Christ's Crucifixion and Adam's deep sleep, then more startling links between the Crucifixion and Noah's drunken stupor. These insights are explored in the sections below, as are further Patristic commentators explaining how Calvary was richly prefigured by Jacob, Moses and Samson.

With such great authorities as these building on the foundation which Christ laid for the Apostles, we can search confidently for more prefigurations of Christ. In this book, sleep is chosen as a theme to indicate the inexhaustibility of the Scriptures, for when we see that a single motif has such great meaning for salvation, then our admiration for the OT increases exponentially. Its human authors could not have been aware of all these interpretations at the time of writing. Of course they knew the literal sense of their words. But the spiritual senses of the texts, as we will see, can only have been by God's arrangement.

It should be obvious it would be beyond human ability to dishonestly create this phenomenon of prefigurations by plotting and scheming over centuries. The only coherent explanation of this unity throughout the OT and NT is that, by God's grace, the authors were honest in recording reality, and reality has unity from God. We only experience a tiny fraction of reality, so the Holy Spirit has provided focus on what matters most through time by guiding the authors of Sacred Scripture to record this event and not that, this detail and not that one, and express it in this way, not that. The only conspiracy behind the Bible was a conspiration of ancient authors and Churchmen breathing the same Holy Spirit. This Spirit says God is concealed: *"Truly, you are a hidden God, the God of Israel, the Saviour…"* yet He means to be found, for *"I have not said… 'Seek me in vain'"* (Is 45:15,19).

If we seek Him, we will find Him. The *Adam* in the title of this book is not primarily our first parent Adam. Rather the *Adam* denoted by the title of this book is the second Adam, Jesus Christ. Jesus is the One Who slept most deeply and woke most miraculously. He is the form of the living, He is the life of all the saints. Therefore He can be found in every saint.

Further, He asks to enter the heart of every Adam, that is every one of us. If we allow Him in, if we die with Him, then we too will wake up from the sleep of death rejoicing to be with Him.

INSPIRATION IN TRIALS

The long list of OT persons who slept in Christ (that is to say, their various sleeps found meaning in Christ) suggests we are all called to sleep in Christ. We are all supposed to undergo our passion with Him. We endure burdens in life which, if willingly accepted, even if they seem senseless at the time, will later be revealed to be salutary. So it was in the OT. So it is now. Jesus instructed us: *"Take up your cross and follow Me"* (Mt 16:24). St Paul put it into practice: *"I have been nailed to the cross with Christ"* (Gal 2:19-20). This is said for our imitation.

Importantly, the best crosses are not those we select for ourselves, but those which circumstances place upon us. Everyone encounters suffering in life, whether sickness, confinement, betrayal, divorce, bereavement. How unbearable it seems at first. But these are opportunities to willingly participate in the Passion. When we offer up our suffering as penance for our sins or for the sake of others, or as reparation for offences against God and Our Lady, then we discover the greatest happiness on earth. St Paul wrote:

> *For now I rejoice in my passion on your behalf, and I complete in my flesh the things that are lacking in the Passion of Christ, for the sake of His Body, which is the Church.* (Col 1:24)

How can St Paul rejoice in suffering? Going beneath the surface to find what is hidden, St Margaret Mary Alacoque wrote:

> If we only understood well the value of the Cross and the happiness of love, the Cross would not be so much avoided,

9

but would be cherished and loved so much that no pleasure would be found except in the Cross, no rest except on the Cross... the one desire of pious souls would be to die on the Cross, despised and abandoned by all. But for this to come to pass pure love must sacrifice and consume our hearts as it sacrificed and consumed That of our good Master.[2]

This is, to say the least, counter-intuitive. Therefore, to help convince us that great goods are laid up in suffering, God has given us the OT. The mystical participations in Jesus' Passion by Joseph, Jonah and Ezekiel were bound up with profound pain, but they reveal the way of salvation. Yet the biblical accounts need not involve suffering. Adam's deep sleep was entirely painless. Of the sixteen examples below, Samson was the only one who actually died in the selected prefiguration. For the rest, the connection is some kind of sleep, a relatable state close to us all, which is a metaphor for death. What the accounts do share is to show God is always with us, guiding events for the sake of salvation, of drawing souls to Heaven.

Each of us can unite ourselves perfectly with Christ's Passion through the Good Friday liturgy and daily Mass. Usually we are helped in this if we have been schooled in suffering. Pain is not our goal, but a pedagogy by which we might learn the love of Christ, a window of understanding into what He endured for us. The result, in a grateful soul, is to be filled with charity through adoring the Crucified. When one carries a cross it is a delight to know it unites us with meek Moses, with heroic Abraham, with Adam our first parent. One becomes alive to *all* human history.

---

[2] St Margaret Mary Alacoque, quoted by Rev. J.A. McMullen, C.SS.R. in *The Love of the Sacred Heart, The Science of Suffering.*

If suffering abandons us, we should thank God for periods of ease. Only let us not think this is how life on earth should always be. If there had never been sin we could expect to abide in a garden of pleasures. But Eden is no longer the centre of the world. Calvary is. Geographically they correspond, though permeated by a different odour: penance is now the way to God. In His mercy God gives us respite, but at some point pain will return to bind us more firmly to the Cross. Study of Sacred Scripture educates us to embrace the bitter wood, all the more convinced as we grow in knowledge that the Cross decodes everything; completes everything; fulfils every story; gives the deepest meaning to the lives of the saints.

The fulfilment of the OT in Christ should open our eyes: what was a mystery is seen to make sense; what seemed superfluous is seen to be crucial; what seemed bizarre is seen to be Wisdom. All this increases our faith that God lovingly governs the faintest details of everything. Truly our lives are in His Hands (Job 12:10; Ps 30:16; 138:10; Is 41:13; Jn 10:28-29), in Whom we are and move and have our being (Acts 17:28). Sense is found not only in our successes but in the otherwise inexplicable, including pain and failures, since:

> we know that, for those who love God, all things work together unto good, for those who, in accordance with His purpose, are called to be saints. (Rom 8:28)

What inflames our heart for Jesus beyond all description? Not that He removes our suffering, but that He fills it with joy. That is divine. It is sweet to suffer for love, as this gives it meaning, in the confidence it will bear fruit. And the highest meaning is to suffer for Christ and His Church, for these are eternal, universal, making the difference for each soul between Heaven and hell. If someone believes their sacrifice will assist others to reach Heaven and avoid hell, then of course they rejoice to suffer for Christ:

Calling in the Apostles, having beaten them, they warned them not to speak at all in the Name of Jesus. And they dismissed them. And... they went forth from the presence of the council, rejoicing that they were considered worthy to suffer insult on behalf of the Name of Jesus. (Acts 5:40-41)

If we have lived in Christ, and died in Him during this earthly life, then we may serenely regard death as truly a falling asleep in the Lord from which we will wake when He returns:

We do not want you to be ignorant, brothers, concerning those who are sleeping, so as not to be sorrowful... For if we believe that Jesus has died and risen again, so also will God bring back with Jesus those who sleep in Him... The dead, who are in Christ, shall rise up first. Next, we who are alive, who are remaining, shall be taken up quickly together with them into the clouds to meet Christ in the air...[and] we shall be with the Lord always. (1 Thes 4:13-17)

Have we strayed? Have we delayed? Are we come late in life to Christ? Take heart: all our experiences have been a formation so that having learned humility, now with maximal trust, with optimal love, if we share Christ's Passion with Noah, Abraham, David and Ezekiel, then we may meet them all merrilie in Heaven! Eternal happiness, or beatitude, is the goal. Suffering is the means. This goal is so good that it injects elation even into the Way of the Cross.

I: Mystical Sleeps
Prefiguring the Passion

I t makes sense that various strange sleeps recorded in the OT point to the Sacrifice of Jesus on Calvary. The ultimate Author of Sacred Scripture, God, uses the word 'sleep' to denote what we call death, because He knows we will wake up from it.[3] Jesus offers this reassurance from His own lips in saying of Jairus' daughter: *"'...the girl is not dead, but asleep.' And they derided Him"* (Mt 9:24). To illustrate the resurrection, Jesus said to her: *"Talitha, koumi"* (Mk 5:41), and so she woke up from death. Again Jesus said: *"Lazarus our friend is sleeping. But I am going, so that I may awaken him from sleep"* (Jn 11:11). Jesus called him out of death. St John Chrysostom observes that Jesus calls death a sleep.[4]

Following Jesus, the Church adopts the same language. St Paul writes: *"But now Christ has risen again from the dead, as the*

---

[3] The OT often uses sleep as a metaphor for death: 1 Kngs 2:10; 11:43; 14:20ss *"he slept with his fathers..."*; Job 3:13; 7:21; 11:18; 2 Macc 12:44-45.

[4] St John Chrysostom, *Homilies on St Matthew's Gospel,* XXXI, 3.

first-fruits of those who sleep" (1 Cor 15:20). St Stephen's bloody passion concludes with the words *"he fell asleep in the Lord"* (Acts 7:59).[5] At the Commemoration of the Dead in each Holy Mass, the Church asks God to remember His servants who *"dormiunt in somno pacis"*, that is "rest in the sleep of peace".[6] We pray: *requiescant in pace.*

Consequently, when we read the Bible and find someone sleeps, this may be God's way of talking about death. We rightly think Adam slept, Noah slept, Jacob slept, but remember: *"Jesus had spoken about his death. Yet they thought that He spoke about the repose of sleep"* (Jn 11:13). At first Jesus' disciples misunderstood. We too misunderstand if when we read of troubled sleeps in the OT we exclude the idea that, while the literal sense has its own value and truth, ultimately God is telling us about death; specifically He wishes to communicate to us about the most significant death of all time — His Son's Passion.

Reading now more carefully, we can find the Crucifixion hidden in the biblical slumbers of Adam, Noah, Abraham, Lot, Abimelech, Isaac, Jacob, Joseph, Moses, Samson, Boaz, Saul, David, Elijah, Jonah, Ezekiel and others. We begin with Adam.

---

[5] Using the same phrase, the Martyrology and Matins frequently tell that a saint *"obdormivit in Domino"*.

[6] Having prayed these words, the priest looks upon the Host as he bows his head in remembrance of persons who have died, as prescribed by the *Ritus servandus*. Soon afterwards when praying the *Our Father*, the priest is instructed again to gaze on the Host, since by looking at Jesus we know the Father: *"who sees Me, sees the Father"* (Jn 14:9). By these two gentle gestures the Church demonstrates her confidence that the faithful departed are living members of Christ, united through Him with the Father, resting peacefully.

THE CROSS IS THE
TREE OF LIFE

The four men considered in this first section — Adam, Noah, Abraham and Jacob — are all principles of life, that is, through them were introduced new kinds of life, and each underwent an arresting participation in the Passion of Christ signified by sleep. Together their experiences suggest the Cross is the source of life for the world, a life far higher than nature or imagination can describe. We might conclude that anyone who would be a principle of life must experience a 'deep sleep', that is a kind of crucifixion.

All human beings are generated from Adam. He is our biological father. God *"has made, out of one, every family of man: to live upon the face of the entire earth"* (Acts 17:26). Noah is the father of all those born after the Flood. Abraham is father of all who live by faith, *"the father of all those who believe... those who are of the faith of Abraham, who is the father of us all before God"* (Rom 4:11-16). Jacob is the father of the twelve tribes of

4 dads - Abraham - By faith
Adam - Biological
Noah - After flood   15
Jacob - 12 tribes

Israel, the People of God. He shows though our life be earthly it is to ascend to the heavenly.

Following on from the mystical crucifixion of these four fathers of life — biological life, blessed life, faith life, heavenly life — there ensued a great multiplication of life. We may infer that each single soul, to reach Heaven, must herself first become a principle of eternal life. This requires being a passive principle before being active. We cannot generate eternal life for ourselves. We can only receive it from God. To be 'passive' is from *pati*, to suffer. It is where we get the word for the Passion. Anyone who would be a principle of life greater than their own — founding a family, or running a school, or to be superior of a monastery, or to found a religious order — does not necessarily have to be crucified. But they have to make sacrifices for their work to be fruitful. They have to accept their share in the Cross.

Passive - Passion
Suffering = Recieved

ADAM'S DEEP SLEEP

God said: 'It is not good for the man to be alone. Let us make a helper for him similar to himself.' Therefore, the Lord God, having formed from the soil all the animals of the earth and all the flying creatures of the air, brought them to Adam, in order to see what he would call them... And Adam called each of the living things by their names... Yet truly, for Adam, there was not found a helper similar to himself. And so the Lord God sent a deep sleep upon Adam. And when he was fast asleep, he took one of his ribs, and he completed it with flesh for it. And the Lord God built up the rib, which he took from Adam, into a woman. And he led her to Adam. And Adam said: 'Now this is bone from my bones, and flesh from my flesh. This one shall be called woman, because she was taken from man.' For this reason, a man shall leave behind his father and mother, and he shall cling to his wife; and the two shall be as one flesh.

— Gen 2:18-24

Why was Eve drawn from Adam's side? Why was she not made from the earth like him? What are the consequences of this original unity? When *"the Lord God sent a deep sleep upon Adam"* (Gen 2:21) it was so that, from man's side, a bride could be made, Eve, who became *"mother of all the living"* (Gen 3:20). St Paul teaches that *"Adam is a figure of Him Who was to come"* (Rom 5:14), namely Jesus. Building on this insight, the greatest doctors of the first and second millennia teach that Eve's origin prefigures the origin of the Church, formed by the supernatural Life which flowed from the New Adam, Jesus Christ, when His

side was opened on the Cross, (Jn 19:34). St Augustine teaches
that as Adam's wife Eve was drawn from his side while sleeping,
so Christ's Bride, the Church, was born from His side in dying.[7]
St Thomas Aquinas explains that beside the unmatched marital,
domestic and social cohesion afforded by the original unity of
Adam and Eve, still the highest reason that Eve was drawn from
Adam is its sacramental signification "that the Church takes her
origin from Christ".[8]

If it seems strange to extrapolate from Adam's painless sleep to
Jesus' agonising death, that is because such thinking is back to
front. We cannot infer the content of the NT by studying only the
OT because the greatness of the events in the NT are too
unexpected. But we can certainly penetrate more deeply into the
OT once it is illumined by Jesus Christ in the NT. The proper
order is to consider what was prior in God's intention. The Son of
God is the Logos through Whom all things are made. Jesus is the
original or the archetype, Adam the print thereof or the type. God
always knew that through His death Jesus would procure the
Church, as there is no greater love, nothing more life-giving, than
to lay down one's life.[9] In order to create an image of this, God
therefore sent a deep sleep upon Adam when fashioning his bride,

---

[7] St Augustine, *Enarration on Psalm 126* and *In Evangelium Ioannis Tractatus*,
CXX, 2 on Jn 19:31ss "the first woman was formed from the side of the man
when asleep, and was called Life, and the mother of all living. Truly it pointed
to a great good… This second Adam bowed His head and fell asleep on the
Cross, that a spouse might be formed for Him from that which flowed from the
sleeper's side. O death, whereby the dead are raised anew to life! What can be
purer than such blood? What more health-giving than such a wound?"

[8] St Thomas Aquinas, *S.Th.* I, Q.92 a.2

life = blood [9] As "*life… is in the blood*" (Lev 17:11), then how great the life which is in
"*the Church of God, which He has purchased by His own Blood*" (Acts 20:28).

18

for sleep is an eloquent metaphor of death. According to St Bonaventura, God *sent* sleep upon Adam in order to *signify* Jesus' death.[10] Such prefigurations demonstrate that God was preparing for the Crucifixion from the beginning.

One of the most striking connections between Jesus and Adam is that they both 'fell asleep', that is died, in the same place. All four Gospels record that Jesus was crucified at *"the place of the skull"*, in Latin "Calvary", in Hebrew "Golgotha".[11] The skull there was Adam's, since it was his burial place.[12] Why did Adam arrange for his family to bury him here? Perhaps because it was the dearest place in the world to him. Adam longed to return to the midst of the garden where he had once been friends with God. Bitterly he regretted his sin. If he returned with Eve to the place of their original fall, this would demonstrate that they were no longer hiding from their guilt but squarely facing it, because there more than anywhere they could see paradise was lost. Recognising the topography, perhaps in this place they taught their sons to offer sacrifice, praying for the promised Messiah to come and conquer death which they knew was coming to them, hoping he would open up the way again to the Tree of Life so that they could *"live in eternity"* (Gen 3:22). It was the place of their happiest memories and their saddest.

---

[10] St Bonaventura, *II Sent.* d.XVIII a.1 q.1, explains Adam slept not because tired, and not because if awake God could not spare him pain and horror in having a rib removed, but because God *sent* sleep upon Adam in order to *signify* Christ's death.

[11] Mt 27:33; Mk 15:22; Lk 23:33; Jn 19:17.

[12] Adam's grave may be visited underneath Calvary in the Church of the Holy Sepulchre in Jerusalem. Icons of the Crucifixion depict Jesus' Precious Blood running down into the rock to reach Adam's skull and redeem him.

In fact, it is the place of all mankind's happiest memories and saddest. Here, Jesus rose to new life from the stone tomb; here, Adam had been taken from the slime of the earth. Here, Jesus fell asleep on the Cross; here, God sent a mystical sleep upon Adam. Here, Eve was generated from Adam's side while sleeping; so, the Church, Christ's Bride, was born from His pierced Heart in dying. Eve was of Adam's bone and flesh with the spirit of God animating her; so the Church is born of the Blood and water which flowed from Christ's side, with the Holy Spirit animating her. Adam was our first father biologically; so Jesus, the New Adam, is our first father spiritually. Eve was our first mother biologically, Adam's helpmate; so Our Lady is our mother spiritually, Christ's Co-Redemptrix, there on Calvary being made Mother of the Church (Jn 19:27), as the first to receive the graces pouring from the Cross.

To review: the place where Adam came into being, *"a living soul"* (Gen 2:7), God also sent upon him a deep sleep. There Adam woke up to see Eve and, a long lifetime later, God sent another deep sleep upon him, his death, at the same place. Here, four thousand years later, the Second Adam died on the Cross; and here woke up in the Resurrection. The two Adams, First and Second, correspond. As Jesus' Precious Blood trickled down to reach the dry skull of Adam, we may understand God's grace reached his soul in limbo, and Adam woke up from death — if not delayed in Purgatory then straight to Heaven. There he saw Eve again, only this time in the true Paradise, their mourning turned to joy, with their children Abel and Seth rejoicing, the promise fulfilled, their friendship with God restored, nevermore to be lost.

What Adam experienced, Jesus magnified. When Jesus came into this world, He was alone, the only Person walking the planet with divine nature. God sent a 'deep sleep' upon Him and when He arose there was His Bride, the Church, beginning with Mary His Mother, then St Mary Magdalene, then St John and the other Apostles. This was now *"bone of my bones and flesh of my flesh"*, for through Faith and His Gift these began sharing also in the divine nature. Now Jesus had company among creatures, human and divine, born from His own side like Adam.

That the origins of human life, Adam sleeping and waking, should have multiple parallels with the origins of our supernatural life, Jesus' dying and rising, is perfectly fitting, given God is the Author of both these beginnings. As the first Adam knew and named every animal, so Jesus knows and names every one of us (Gen 2:18-23; Apoc 2:17; 3:5). As Adam found *"no helper similar to himself"* among the animals, but only in Eve, so Jesus found none who believed in His highest work before it began, except His Mother Mary. *"Helper"* means a partner in the work fit for man, that is suitable for our rational nature. Rational is the key here because when God brought all the animals to Adam, he could not find a collaborator for his proper, ultimate work. He was alone. But when God made woman from him, and brought her to him, Adam rejoiced: *"Now this is bone from my bones, and flesh from my flesh"* (Gen 2:23). Communion began!

What was the work of Adam and Eve, that they would achieve together in communion? Certainly it began in procreating many more humans (*"Increase and multiply"* Gen 1:28), but the highest work of humans is to know God, to praise and to adore Him. Pope John Paul II submits in *Love and Responsibility* that it was looking into Eve's eyes that Adam immediately saw she was different from all the animals, for in each others' eyes both could see they had interior lives, that is rational souls, the faculties of intellect and will. This necessarily means — as they both understood — having an immortal spirit, which is the very image of God. Precisely this constitution enables man to know God in a way the animals cannot. Beasts perceive only particulars, not knowing universals, nor have they free will with which to adore. Eve, however, has the same higher faculties as Adam, so together they can do their proper work. Scripture tells us this work is to worship:

> *He created from him a helper, similar to himself. He gave them counsel, and language, and sight, and hearing, and a heart, in order to think. And he filled them with the discipline of understanding. He created within them the knowledge of the spirit. He filled their heart with understanding, and he showed them both good and evil. He set his eye upon their hearts, to reveal to them the greatness of his works, so that they might highly praise the name of sanctification, and give glory to his wonders, so that they might declare the greatness of his works.* (Sir 17:5-8)

Now the work of Adam and Eve in Eden was perfected by Jesus and Mary. In the beginning, the worship of Adam and Eve consisted in obeying the commandment not to eat of the Tree of Life. So it is for everybody: *"if you wish to enter into life, observe the commandments"* (Mt 19:17). St Ephraim writes that God intended to give Adam and Eve the fruit of the Tree of Life but only after they had first proved their obedience.[13] Had they done this, they would have been awarded immortality. Instead through disobedience they fell, some Fathers deducing it was on the very

---

[13] St Ephraim, *Commentary on Genesis,* II, 17; 18; 31; 35.

day they were created.[14] As early as the second generation, Cain's offering was not pleasing to God (Gen 4:5). The increase of life God commanded was turned by the same Cain to murder, a theme for the world ever since. Subsequent generations, turning a fall into a dive, practised idolatry. But to rescue our species from failure, to offer God His due and as commanded give an increase of life, in time came Mary and Jesus. In the same centre of Eden, now called Calvary, Jesus offered perfect worship to God, accomplishing on the Cross a Sacrifice which would please Him for eternity. And who else was present to fully assist at this offering but the Blessed Virgin Mary, surpassing obedience in giving to God that which pleased Him most: His Son.[15] Because of her loving cooperation on Calvary, the Mother of God becomes also mother of all God's children, a new *"mother of all the living"* (Gen 3:20), wherefore the Son of God tells us: *"Behold thy mother."* (Jn 19:27)

Though is it Mary as Mother, or the Church, who is the New Eve, born from Christ's pierced heart? It is both, in that on Calvary Mary was the living Church, the only living member, and became the Mother of the entire Church. Adam and Eve began as one flesh, and came together as one flesh in order that new life proceed. So the Church proceeds from Christ, each member reuniting with Him as one spirit, so that eternal life proceed. Mary was the first to unite with Him in spirit.

---

[14] St Irenæus, *Adversus Haereses*, V, 23, 2.

[15] St Irenæus, *Adversus Haereses*, III, 22, 1-4, tells us that as Jesus is the New Adam Who recapitulates Creation after it was disordered by the sin of the first Adam, so the Blessed Virgin Mary is the New Eve who undoes the knot tied by the first Eve. See also St Justin Martyr, *Dialogue with Trypho*, 100.

Adam then was the principle of our biological life, and by disobedience the principle of our death. Jesus Christ is the principle of our spiritual life, by obedience (Phil 2:8) overturning death into eternal life.

> *Therefore, just as through the offence of one, all men fell under condemnation, so also through the justice of one, all men fall under justification unto life. For, just as through the disobedience of one man, many were established as sinners, so also through the obedience of one man, many shall be established as just.* (Rom 5:18-19)

The Tree of Life stands at the centre of all this. St John, who stood there, wrote that those who enter Heaven *"wash their robes in the blood of the Lamb: that they may have a right to the tree of life and may enter in by the gates into the city"* (Apoc 22:14). To *"wash... in the blood of the Lamb"* means to be sanctified by the Sacrifice of Jesus, for example in Baptism or Confession. These Sacraments gain us *"a right to the tree of life"*, that is to take the fruit which hangs on the Cross, namely the Body of Christ. If we receive the Holy Eucharist worthily, we *"enter in by the gates into the city"*, Heaven. Jesus is the principle of life for the world.

> *I am the living bread, Who descended from heaven. If anyone eats from this bread, he shall live in eternity. And the bread that I will give is My Flesh, for the life of the world.* (Jn 6:51-52)

NOAH'S DRUNKEN STUPOR

And so the sons of Noah, who came out of the ark, were Shem, Ham, and Japheth. Now Ham himself is the father of Canaan. These three are the sons of Noah. And from these all the family of mankind was spread over the whole earth. And Noah, a good farmer, began to cultivate the land, and he planted a vineyard. And by drinking its wine, he became inebriated and was naked in his tent. Because of this, when Ham, the father of Canaan, had indeed seen the privates of his father to be naked, he reported it to his two brothers outside. And truly, Shem and Japheth put a cloak upon their arms, and, advancing backwards, covered the privates of their father. And their faces were turned away, so that they did not see their father's manhood. Then Noah, awaking from the wine, when he had learned what his younger son had done to him, he said, 'Cursed be Canaan, a servant of servants will he be to his brothers.' And he said: 'Blessed be the Lord God of Shem, let Canaan be his servant. May God enlarge Japheth, and may he live in the tents of Shem, and let Canaan be his servant.'

— Gen 9:18-27

Why does Genesis tell us that Noah got drunk? Why was he spread flat out naked? Certainly by his life's work Noah prefigures Jesus. The Torah emphasises by stating threefold: *"Noah did all that God commanded him"* (Gen 6:8,22; 7:5), and Jesus did all that God sent Him to do,[16] both thereby saving the

---

[16] Jn 14:31; 15:10,15; 17:7-8; 19:28. Jesus, being God, expects the same obedience of His disciples: Mt 28:20; Lk 17:10.

world, of course at different levels. Given Noah was the first man to cultivate wine, he can be excused any moral fault in his unwittingly becoming inebriated. But as God determined before all Creation that wine would be the chosen sign for Jesus' Most Precious Blood, then Noah being the first person ever to pour wine represents Christ pouring out His Blood. Noah naked and inebriated signifies the Passion of Christ.

The Prophet Jeremiah employs the imagery of inebriation to signify death:

> *In their heat, I will give them a drink, and I will inebriate them, so that they become drowsy, and sleep an everlasting sleep, and do not rise up, says the Lord... And I will inebriate her leaders, and her wise ones, and her military rulers, and her civil rulers, and her strong ones. And they will sleep an everlasting sleep, and they will not awaken, says the King: the Lord of Hosts...* (Jer 51:39,57)

The repeated phrase *"sleep an everlasting sleep"* evidently means death. The Prophet Isaiah also relates drunkenness to death, yet which God Himself will take away:

> *Lift up, Lift up! Arise, O Jerusalem! You drank, from the hand of the Lord, the cup of his wrath. You drank, even to the bottom of the cup of deep sleep. And you were given to drink, all the way to the dregs... There is devastation and destruction, and famine and sword... Your sons have been cast out. They have slept at the head of all the roads... Therefore, listen to this, O poor little ones, and you who have been inebriated, but not by wine. Thus says your Sovereign, the Lord, and your God, who will fight on behalf*

of his people: Behold, I have taken the cup of deep sleep
from your hand. You shall no longer drink from the bottom
of the cup of my indignation. (Is 51:17-22)

Therefore, Jesus, to take our punishment on Himself, told Peter to put away his sword: *"Should I not drink the chalice which My Father has given to Me?"* (Jn 18:11) Jesus drank *"from the bottom of the cup"*, the last hellish dregs, to spare us from them.

Going deeper, St Augustine understands the vineyard Noah planted to signify Israel, the People whom God planted, yet who rebelled against Him (Is 5; Mt 21:33-46). So Noah becoming drunk from the work of his own hands denotes the humiliation of Christ at the hands of His own people, whom as God He planted:

> Again the sufferings of Christ from His own nation are
> evidently denoted by Noah being drunk with the wine of the
> vineyard he planted, and his being uncovered in his tent.
> For the mortality of Christ's flesh was uncovered, to the
> Jews a stumbling-block, and to the Greeks foolishness; but
> to them that are called, both Jews and Greeks, both Shem
> and Japheth, the power of God and the wisdom of God...[17]

The nakedness of Noah pre-echoes Christ's nakedness on the Cross: the Son of God had assumed human flesh like a garment, which was stripped from Him on Calvary. The simple nakedness of being without clothing signifies the awful nakedness of the person when the body is separated from the soul in death. Ham laughed at his father's nakedness, but his two brothers reverently covered it up. So St Augustine citing St Paul above explains that the notion that God should take on mortal flesh and die is rejected

---

[17] St Augustine, *Contra Faustum*, XII, 23.

as incomprehensible by some Jews and Gentiles ("Greeks"), but embraced as a divine mystery by other Jews and Gentiles. In another place St Augustine writes:

> But Shem and Japheth, that is to say, the circumcision and uncircumcision, or, as the apostle otherwise calls them, the Jews and Greeks, but called and justified, having somehow discovered the nakedness of their father (which signifies the Saviour's Passion), took a garment and laid it upon their backs, and entered backwards and covered their father's nakedness, without their seeing what their reverence hid. For we both honour the Passion of Christ as accomplished for us, and we hate the crime of the Jews who crucified Him. The garment signifies the sacrament, their backs the memory of things past: for the church celebrates the Passion of Christ as already accomplished, and no longer to be looked forward to, now that Japheth already dwells in the habitations of Shem, and their wicked brother between them... [Noah] drinks of its wine... by which He obviously means His Passion... *'and he was drunken'*, that is, He suffered; *'and was naked'*, that is, His weakness appeared in His suffering...[18]

---

[18] St Augustine, *De Civitate Dei,* XVI, 2, continuing: "when to the expression *'he was naked'* Scripture adds *'in his house,'* it elegantly intimates that Jesus was to suffer the Cross and death at the hands of His own household, His own kith and kin, the Jews. This Passion of Christ is only externally and verbally professed by the reprobate, for what they profess, they do not understand. But the elect hold in the inner man this so great mystery, and honour inwardly in the heart this weakness and foolishness of God. And of this there is a figure in Ham going out to proclaim his father's nakedness; while Shem and Japheth, to cover or honour it, went in, that is to say, did it inwardly."

So an episode which seems strange on first reading is unpacked to reveal the most important event in history. The Passion of Christ is prefigured in naked Noah.[19] The reaction of his sons includes Jews and Gentiles united in reverence for His Sacrifice. A wonderful interpretation is given to the two brothers walking backwards: namely, they proceed together with their naked father behind them, meaning the Passion of Christ is now in the past, but they laid a garment to cover Noah, as Jesus is veiled in the Holy Eucharist. Or else it indicates that we all walk backwards through time, for we cannot see what is coming in the future, but we can look back on the past. Those who lived before the Crucifixion could not see it, but those of us who come after have it always before our eyes.

The observation that "Japheth already dwells in the habitations of Shem" means Christians live in tabernacles of the elder brother, the Jews. That is, our life in the New Covenant fulfils and does not abolish the framework of the Old. Our Catholic tabernacles fulfil the tabernacle of Moses as the place to encounter God.

Could Noah ever have guessed his drunkenness would one day be raised to such a noble cause! Truly our God is a God Who unites opposites, who makes sense of the senseless.

Offering another interpretation, St Jerome sees Noah's planting of the vineyard not as God establishing Israel but as Christ planting the Church:

> When Noah left the ark he planted a vineyard, drank thereof, and was drunken. Christ also, born in the flesh, planted the Church and suffered. The elder son made sport

---

[19] We recall Adam was also naked in his sleep (Gen 2:25).

of his father's nakedness, the younger covered it: and the Jews mocked God crucified, the Gentiles honoured Him.[20]

Jesus is the true vine, the faithful are His branches (Jn 15:1-8). In this reading, the wine therefrom is not thought of as a bloody execution but as a most precious gift: Noah's wine represents the Blood of Christ as flowing for all generations from the chalice in Holy Mass. Accordingly, in the Sistine Chapel Michelangelo painted a recumbent Noah opposite a bloody Levitical oblation, thereby indicating Noah's sleep also has a sacrificial character.

The three sons of Noah taken together — Shem, Ham and Japheth — stand for all mankind (Gen 9:18). They are blessed or cursed by their father Noah, or rather by God, depending upon their reaction to the Cross. Truly whoever shows reverence for Christ's Sacrifice leads the blessed life, while to hold it in contempt is to be miserable.[21] It does not matter if one is rich and powerful, or poor and afflicted. What is decisive is whether or not

---

[20] St Jerome, *Altercatio Luciferiani et Orthodoxi*, 22.

[21] As Ham sinned against his father, why was it that Noah cursed Ham's son Canaan rather than Ham himself? Perhaps to show that whatever was good in Ham was not cursed, but that in him which opposed God's plan. Ham had four sons: *"the sons of Ham were Cush, and Mizraim, and Put, and Canaan"* (Gen 10:6). These respectively indicate those who settled in Ethiopia, Egypt, Libya and Canaan (later Israel). It was the descendants of the last who most directly opposed God's people, earning their curse.

Or as St Ambrose writes, a noble father (like Noah) can have a degenerate son (like Ham), but a degenerate son who rebels against his noble father is incapable of bringing up a noble son (*Treatise on Noah*, XXX). This is an image of the perfect Father, God, having a son who chose degeneracy (Adam), thus causing a 'curse' to fall on his descendants (original sin).

Thanks be to God, in Jesus Christ the sons can be reborn (Jn 3:5-6; 1 Pet 1:23) and need not pay for the sins of the fathers (Jer 31:29-34; Ezek 18:2-32; 2 Cor 5:10; 1 Pet 1:17-19. Also St Justin Martyr, *Dialogue with Trypho,* 139-140).

one is grateful to God. Ultimately, this leads to Heaven or hell, for Judgement hangs on the Cross. As one-third laughed and was cursed, so two-thirds were respectful and blessed. This may remind us of the angels: one-third of them fell, while two-thirds enjoy Heaven (cf. Apoc 12:4).

What the great Latin Fathers taught about Noah's drunken sleep is mirrored in the East by the poetry of St Ephraim the Syrian. He composed a dispute between Death and satan wherein satan claims that although on the ark the mighty Noah overcame global death, still satan was able to humiliate Noah through excess of wine. But Death retorts that the devil injures ultimately only his own, here hurting Ham, while Noah's very humiliation was turned to glory — as the series of verses shows — in Christ's Crucifixion, where putting on weakness was turned to power:

Narrator: I heard Death and satan, as they disputed… Listen, my brethren, to Death, mocking the Evil One: that caused the head of our race to sin, and its mother…

satan: Noah who conquered the flood, as it were death: by the mouth of Ham I laughed at, when wine overcame him.

Death: Noah was not harmed, but your garment, wherewith you clothed him: even cursings, he put on, and became a slave [*i.e.* Ham].[22]

We have seen multiple Church Fathers interpret Noah's drunken torpor as Christ's Passion. These men were close to the Apostles in time, in mind and in heart. Without them we could scarcely understand what the Scriptures mean. Aware now that

---

[22] St Ephraim, *Nisibene Hymns*, LVII.

Adam's sleep and Noah's sleep each foreshadow Calvary, we are more likely to pause and ponder the next time we find 'sleep' in the Scriptures. As God is eager to communicate more, we do not have long to wait.

ABRAM'S DREAD DARKNESS

The Lord responded to Abram: 'Take for me a cow of three years, and a she-goat of three years, and a ram of three years, also a turtle-dove and a pigeon.' Taking all these, he divided them through the middle, and placed both parts opposite one another. But the birds he did not divide. And birds descended upon the carcasses, but Abram drove them away. And when the sun was setting, a deep sleep fell upon Abram, and a dread, great and dark, invaded him. And it was said to him: 'Know beforehand that your future offspring will be sojourners in a land not their own, and they will subjugate them in servitude and afflict them for four hundred years. Yet truly, I will judge the nation that they will serve, and after this they will depart with great substance. But you will go to your fathers in peace and be buried at a good old age. But in the fourth generation, they will return here. For the iniquities of the Amorites are not yet completed, even to this present time.' Then, when the sun had set, there came a dark mist, and there appeared a smoking furnace and a lamp of fire passing between those divisions. On that day, God formed a covenant with Abram, saying: 'To your offspring I will give this land...'

— Gen 15:9-19

While cutting a covenant with God, Abram saw the New Covenant within it. Abram separated animal parts as a sacrifice, physically cutting his own covenant with God, and during the course of this he saw moving through the divisions a vision of a

lamp=Jesus
fire=Triune God

lamp and a fire. God was showing to Abram the deeper reality to which their own covenant pointed: namely the New and Eternal Covenant sealed in sacrifice by Jesus Christ (the lamp) and the Triune God (the fire). The actions and words of the OT are pregnant with meaning because they carry within them the NT. In due course God's covenantal promises to Abram would bear something greater than any man had guessed — divinity.

Thirteen chapters after Adam's deep sleep, and six after Noah's, another sleep is described within perhaps the most mysterious episode in the Torah. *"And when the sun was setting, a deep sleep fell upon Abram, and a dread, great and dark, invaded him"* (Gen 15:12). The phrase *"deep sleep"* reminds us of that which God caused to fall upon Adam (Gen 2:21). In the Vulgate, St Jerome uses the word *sopor* for both sleeps, an unnatural lethargy from which it is difficult to rise. The Septuagint has ἔκστασις for both, an ecstasy, being outside of oneself. The Hebrew has תַּרְדֵּמָה, meaning dormancy, or hibernation, a word used only twice in the Torah: first for Adam and now for Abram.[23] Does God want us to draw a link between the experiences of the two men? Yes, because just as Adam's *"deep sleep"* points to the Passion and the generation of the Church, so also the whole of Genesis 15 speaks about the Passion and the generation of the Church, this time not under the aspect of a bride, but as consisting in myriads of God's children.

The chapter begins with God promising an heir to Abram who will issue from his own body, then numerous descendants, and to these will be given land for a possession (Gen 15:1*ff*). Now the heir, the number of descendants, and the land they will inherit, are

---

[23] תַּרְדֵּמָה is used just seven times in the whole Tanakh: Gen 2:21; 15:12; 1 Sam 26:12; Job 4:13; 33:15; Prov 19:15; Is 29:10.

all far more awesome than we might at first think. The heir is Jesus Christ, the Son of God and son of Abraham.[24] As for his descendants, God notified Abram: *"'Take in the heavens, and number the stars, if you can... So shall your offspring be.' Abram believed God..."* (Gen 15:5-6). Today, billions of baptised souls have Abraham as their father in Faith.[25] Abram was worried that the son of his steward, Eliezer of Damascus, would be his heir, but God reassured him that his heir would come from his own loins (Gen 15:2-4). The familial bond of father and son signifies that in Jesus Christ we inherit the Kingdom of God not merely as servants, that is as creatures made by God, but as true sons of God. For in Baptism we are truly born in Christ, that is supernaturally adopted in the Only Begotten Son in such a way that supersedes all social and legal forms of adoption. It is ontological, meaning by Baptism we actually begin to partake in the divine Nature. This adoption by grace is more real than biological sonship.

As the sonship in Christ is better than that sonship of Abraham, so the inheritance through Christ is better than Abraham's. The land promised to Abraham was that where he stood conversing with God (Gen 15:7), identified as lying *"from the river of Egypt even to the great river Euphrates"* (Gen 15:18). On a material level this is Israel, populated stage by stage, but unstable. Given land is what we live from, it is a metaphor for a soul; and a country is a metaphor for a union of souls; and the Holy Land a metaphor for Heaven itself. So the true fulfilment and

---

[24] Mk 1:1; Mt 1:1; Lk 3:23-38.

[25] *"...it is from faith according to grace that the Promise is ensured for all the seed, not only for those who are of the law, but also for those who are of the faith of Abraham, who is the father of us all..."* (Rom 4:11-16).

[handwritten margin notes: Land = Soul / Country = Union of Souls / Holy Land = Heaven]

permanence of this promise is in Jesus Christ. In Him is the everlasting inheritance of the saints. He abides in us and we abide in Him. It is Jesus, by His Resurrection from the dead, Who like Joshua leads us over the river of death into the Promised Land.

Hence the fulfilment of God's promises exceeds what we can conceive. Abraham fathered not only a son (Isaac), but the Son of God. Abraham has had not only millions upon millions of biological descendants through Isaac, but billions upon billions of spiritual descendants through Jesus Christ. And the land inherited by them is not just a patch of territory east of the Mediterranean, nor even is it confined to the whole world with the spread of the Church, but it is Heaven itself, participation in God. The saints dwell in God. When God promises, He does not disappoint.

These promises of an heir, of countless descendants, and of a place to dwell, are guaranteed through sacrifice (Gen 15:8-10). The meaning of the animals being cut in two and their pieces laid out upon the ground is for the sealing of a covenant in blood, a vivid sign of the price to be paid if the covenant is broken. The parties walking between the divided parts of the animals serves as a signature to the deal, an unforgettable act marking voluntary assent and staking one's being upon it, both attesting that they are willing to be cut in two if they would ever dare to violate the agreement: 'May God do so to me and more if...' That Abram's covenant with God is cut in bloody sacrifice prepares us for Calvary. This is the heart of the matter.

When *"the sun was setting"* comes the *"deep sleep... a dread, great and dark, invaded him"* (Gen 15:12). So is depicted our Spiritual Sun, Jesus Christ, descending into death. Vividly the Vulgate has *"horror magnus et tenebrosus invasit eum"*. We can all see *"horror"* means "horror"; we might know *"magnus"* means "great" (think magnitude, magnificent, magnate, Magnificat); whoever has prayed *Tenebrae* during the night for Easter or Christmas might recognise *"tenebrosus"* means "darkness"; and *"invasit"* is clearly an invasion, indicating something hostile which comes within from without, an evil force. Abram's sleep is portentous. The equivalent Septuagint text includes "φόβος", meaning "fear" (as in phobia); "μέγας", meaning "great" (as in mega); "σκοτεινὸς" used elsewhere for the "darkness" of death (Homer) or of the netherworld (Pindar) or of ignorance (Plato); and "επιπίπτει" as used in the previous chapter for Abram himself in battle *"falling upon"* or *"rushing upon"* and wasting the four kings who had kidnapped his nephew Lot (Gen 14:15), as in a military assault.

All this paints the picture of what Abram experienced: being overrun by fearful and total void. In the Hebrew the אֵימָה (dread terror) and חֲשֵׁכָה (darkness) make their first appearance in the Torah here. Nothing so grim had yet befallen a man. Abram was truly tested.

With good reason, God's arrangement with Abram was bound up with enormous affliction, because before Abram's seed would enter the land, centuries of slavery and suffering would have to be endured (Gen 15:13-17). Literally, this was the ever crueller subjugation of the Hebrews under pharaoh until the Exodus. Interpreted, we may think of the Church's tribulations on earth before her assumption into Heaven. More vitally, the passage indicates that the Promised Seed — Jesus Christ — would undergo His agonising Passion, bearing the sins of the world. Entry into the land would not occur until *"the iniquities of the Amorrhites"* were full (Gen 15:16). The sins of man were full when we crucified God; straight after this, the heavenly homeland was opened. This may all be recapitulated in the end days if the sins of the world fill up again as Judgement Day approaches.

To encourage us all, God told Abram: *"Yet truly, I will judge the nation that they will serve, and after this they will depart with great substance"* (Gen 12:14). The enslaving powers of this world will finally be judged while we who count Abraham as our father will emerge from death *"with great substance"*. Substance may mean goods, property, wealth, herds, livelihood, or money in the bank. All these stand for life, as also our food is our substance. Ultimately though, our substance is our being, and to come out of death with *"great substance"* means to share in the Risen Life of Jesus Christ, our very being enriched with divinity. No substance is greater. No better fulfilment of the promises to Abram could even be imagined. So the sufferings of this present age are not worthy to be compared with the glory to come.

The way to future glory from this present age with its inevitable sufferings is through sacrifice:

> *Then, when the sun had set, there came a dark mist, and there appeared a smoking furnace and a lamp of fire passing between the divisions.* (Gen 15:17)

Passing between the *"divisions"* is between the pieces of the victims. Precisely when God is cutting a Covenant with Abram, Abram has a vision of another Covenant. He sees a Covenant within the Covenant. Both involve sacrifice and blessing.

The exterior Covenant which Abram was making with God promised biological descendants and land made literally of stones and soil. But the interior Covenant which he saw promised a way to prevail over death, as surely as light over darkness. This is part of the meaning of the fire-pot and the torch which Abram witnessed passing between the divisions. The significance of fire and light is the Holy Trinity and the Incarnate Son, and their cutting an eternal Covenant together. Jesus said: *"I am the light of the world"* (Jn 8:12; 9:5; 12:46). He is the *"true Light"* (Jn 1:9), the very meaning of 'light'. As for the fire, *"our God is a consuming fire"* (Dt 4:24; 9:3; Heb 12:29). The fiery furnace into which Shadrach, Meshach and Abednego were cast represents God, where the blessed live unhurt, singing the divine praises (Dan 3:23-45; 51-90), while their persecutors are incinerated upon approach (Dan 3:48). Peering into this furnace King Nebuchadnezzar declared:

> *Behold, I see four men unbound and walking in the midst of the fire, and no harm is in them, and the appearance of the fourth is like a son of God.* (Dan 3:93)

Surely here is a vision of the Incarnate Lord Jesus, at home in the Blessed Trinity. Such is the highest meaning of fire.

So while Abram made a temporal covenant with God, there in the midst of it, as if perceiving its ultimate meaning, he saw a deal being sealed between God and the God-man, a commitment which therefore could never be broken, given the two signatory parties were both perfect. God is obviously perfect. And as perfect Man, Jesus ratifies on behalf of man the Covenant with God. In Jesus Christ God signed the agreement. That is, God swore by Himself, as He would again at Isaac's binding: *"God, in making promises to Abraham, swore by Himself, because He had no one greater by whom He might swear"* (Heb 6:12-13; cf. Gen 22:16). Contemplating the Old Covenant, we can by God's grace see the New concealed within it. Abram was the first to glimpse this.

In Faith, Abraham saw Christ, his own seed, there in the midst of death, of sacrifice, yet living, and passing through. It was when the sun had set that Abram saw the light of Christ, the lamp of fire; as many of us come to know Jesus when life is at its darkest. Because he has faith in Christ, *"on that day, God cut a covenant with Abram"* (Gen 15:18). Although night has fallen, the Scripture calls this *"day"*, since Abraham rejoiced to see Christ's *"Day"* (Jn 8:56). He rejoiced for the light he saw burning so brightly speaks of the glory of Christ through the centuries, the glory of all the Holy Masses offered as testament to the glory of the Cross, the pouring of Blood in the New and Eternal Covenant.[26]

Moreover, God, as Most Holy Trinity and as Incarnate Son, divided not mere animals but divided the darkness — meaning the defeat of irrationality and death. Fittingly, each Requiem Mass pleads that the departed soul be brought "into the holy light which You once promised to Abraham and his seed".[27]

But what of those who are engulfed by darkness, who are not delivered from the pains of hell, the deep pit, the lion's mouth? The manifestation of a covenant not kept is carcasses being devoured by beasts and birds, which symbolises demons taking away the souls of the unfaithful (cf. Mt 13:4,19).

And I will give over the men who have betrayed my covenant, and who have not observed the words of the covenant, to which they assented in my sight when they cut

---

[26] Jesus' 'Hour' was His Passion. His 'Day' is His Glorified Life. See Heb 4:6-10 for an indication that 'day' means heavenly rest.

[27] *Missa defunctorum, Offertorium, "...in lucem sanctam: Quam olim Abrahæ promisisti et semini eius."*

the calf into two parts and passed between its parts: the leaders of Judah, and the leaders of Jerusalem, the eunuchs and the priests, and all the people of the land, who have passed between the parts of the calf. And I will give them into the hands of their enemies and into the hands of those who are seeking their life. And their dead bodies will be food for the birds of the air and for the beasts of the earth. (Jer 34:18-20)

But if you are not willing to listen to the voice of the Lord your God, so as to keep and do all his commandments and ceremonies, which I instruct to you this day, all these curses shall come to you... May your carcass be food for all the flying things of the air and the wild beasts of the land, and may there be no one to drive them away. (Dt 28:15,26)

The horrible image of corpses being devoured by the birds and beasts signifies damnation, of being tormented and consumed even after death. This unlocks those enigmatic words, written about Abram's faith in the Christ to come: *"And when the fowls came down upon the carcasses, Abram drove them away"* (Gen 15:11). This was ultimately about Jesus' Passion, and Jesus was not devoured in death. Specifically, no demon reached His divinity, neither did His soul become ensnared by hell, nor did His Body see corruption (Ps 15:10; Acts 2:21; 13:35). Though His Body, Blood and Soul were separated from each other in death, each remained united with His Divinity, and all were perfectly reunited in His glorious Resurrection. This is most important to Abram, who, representing the Father, drove the birds and beasts away from the parts of the sacrifice.

What does our father Abraham wish to communicate to us above all else? Belief in the Resurrection. This is his greatness: faith unto the end. Where did Abraham get this Faith stronger than death? Surely it is connected with his leaving his homeland and surviving, even prospering; and with his going down to Egypt and escaping perilous threats; going north to rescue Lot and triumphing against the odds. We do not know the details of his experiences, but perhaps if he repeatedly escaped death by God's aid then he came to know God was with him, for him. This trust became so strong that Abraham even believed death was not the end, that though his own beloved son should die on Mount Moriah, yet he would live again and prosper.

So Abraham was successively schooled to perfect his faith in Christ. His willingness to offer his son, his only-begotten, his beloved, Isaac, was the single greatest act of any human being in the OT. He believed in resurrection, God's gift, indestructible life.

To identify Abram as the principle of the life of faith does not mean that he is the beginning of it in the sense that none beforehand had faith. Noah did. Enoch did. Abel did. Rather, Abraham's faith in the Resurrection points perfectly to Jesus Christ, Who is the real principle of faith for absolutely everyone who believes, even reaching backwards in time to all those who awaited Him with hope, who expected Him, reaching even Adam and Eve who believed in the Seed of the woman. Many believed weakly or vaguely, but Abraham believed God so strongly he was willing to give his son. This makes Abraham our father in faith. His name begins with 'father' (Gen 17:5). Like no one else in the OT he points us to God the Father.

When Jesus Christ came, He revealed the Father perfectly. So much does the Father love us, as to send His own Son to die for us. Jesus cut a New Covenant in His own Blood. Whosoever of us enters this Covenant, believing in His Promises as Abraham believed, will inherit the Promised Land, the Heavenly Jerusalem, eternal life, in communion with billions upon billions of angels and saints, with Abraham, Isaac and, in the centre, Jesus Himself.

JACOB'S AWESOME SLEEP

*When Jacob had arrived at a certain place, where he would
rest after the setting of the sun, he took some of the stones
that lay there, and placing them under his head, he slept in
the same place. And he saw in his sleep: a ladder standing
upon the earth, with its top touching heaven, also, the
Angels of God ascending and descending by it, and the
Lord, leaning upon the ladder, saying to him: 'I am the
Lord, the God of Abraham your father, and the God of
Isaac. The land, in which you sleep, I will give to you and to
your seed. And your seed will be like the dust of the earth.
You will spread abroad to the West, and to the East, and to
the North, and to the Meridian. And in you and in your
seed, all the tribes of the earth shall be blessed. And I will
be your guardian wherever you will journey, and I will
bring you back into this land. Neither will I dismiss you,
until I have accomplished all that I have said.' And when
Jacob had awakened from sleep, he said, 'Truly, the Lord is
in this place, and I did not know it.' And being terrified, he
said: 'How terrible this place is! This is nothing other than
the house of God and the gateway of heaven.' Therefore,
Jacob, arising in the morning, took the stone which he had
placed under his head, and he set it up as a monument,
pouring oil over it. And he called the name of the city,
'Bethel,' which before was called Luz. And then he made a
vow, saying: 'If God will be with me, and will guard me
along the way by which I walk, and will give me bread to
eat and clothing to wear, and if I will return prosperously to
my father's house, then the Lord will be my God, and this*

stone, which I have set up as a monument, will be called "the House of God". And from all the things that you will give to me, I will offer tithes to you.'

— Gen 28:11-22

This passage is packed with profundity. Jacob's dream may be interpreted as a remote vision of Holy Mass. The setting is the house of God, anticipating each church building. The rock represents Jesus; its anointing with oil announces He is the Messiah; placed in the house of God it stands for the altar.[28] Jacob resting his head on the rock and sleeping signifies the heads or leaders of God's People — priests — sharing in Christ's Passion: this they do at the altar not by dying (sleeping) but by offering Holy Mass, the memorial of the Crucifixion. As Jacob in his sleep had a vision of a ladder adorned with angels ascending to and descending from the heavens, so the invisible reality of Holy Mass is the Sacrifice of the Cross which opens the way to Heaven. Souls who assist at Holy Mass may be served by angels ascending who carry our prayers and raise our minds and hearts heavenward, and by angels descending to comfort and instruct us. How is all this so?

Introducing this episode, the Scripture tells us Abraham's grandson Jacob, *"having departed from Beersheba, continued on to Haran"* (Gen 28:10). This is the reverse journey which Abram made when God called him. If Abram's descent from Haran represents Christ's Incarnation (cf. Acts 7:2-3), then perhaps

---

[28] The Office of Matins for the Dedication of the Archbasilica of Our Holy Saviour (9th Nov), *Lectio IV*, observes that Jacob setting up an Altar for a pillar and pouring chrism thereon gives "a figure of our Lord Jesus Christ, Who is Himself our Altar, our Victim, and our Priest."

Jacob's return journey northwards, passing by Bethlehem, Jerusalem and Bethel, may somehow trace out Christ's Birth (Bethlehem), Passion (Jerusalem) and Ascension (Bethel),[29] the whole Pascal Mystery? Jacob made this journey to seek a wife. Corresponding to this, the reason for Jesus' Mission was to establish the Church, His Bride.

What happened during Jacob's journey to accomplish his mission? He lay down to sleep on a rock outside Jerusalem and had a vision of a ladder reaching Heaven, with angels ascending and descending, *"and the Lord, leaning upon the ladder"*. Here, God renewed the promises of the Covenant. All this speaks of Jesus and the New Covenant.

Upon waking Jacob said, trembling: *"How terrible this place is! This is nothing other than the house of God and the gateway of heaven"* (Gen 28:16-17).[30] Hence the place was called Beth-el: the House of God.[31] Rabbinic traditions say this is where the Temple was later built. Certainly the Temple was God's House. But can this be the fulfilment of the whole incident, its final meaning?

St Irenæus, leaning on the Apostles, teaches that the ladder signifies the Cross [see footnote 29]. He references Isaiah that no earthly habitation (no stone temple) is sufficient for the Godhead,

---

[29] St Irenæus, *Demonstrations of the Apostolic Preaching,* XLV "And Jacob, when he went into Mesopotamia, saw Him in a dream, standing upon the ladder, that is the tree which was set up from earth to heaven; for thereby they that believe in Him go up to the heavens. For His sufferings are our ascension on high..."

[30] Dedication of a Church, *Introitus: "Terribilis est locus iste: hic domus Dei est et porta caeli: et vocabitur aula Dei."*

[31] How can one stone represent the House of God? Because the altar is more essential to worship than the whole building.

and further explains Christ's descending into suffering is our ascending into eternal life. The Cross gives access to Heaven. Hence God renewing the promises of the Covenant in Jacob's dream, in his sleep (Gen 28:13-15), points to the New Covenant established in Jesus' Passion and Death.

St Justin Martyr beforehand and countless commentators from East and West after him also identify the ladder with the Cross of Calvary, and then the stone Jacob anointed with oil stands for the Rock, the Messiah, Jesus Christ, anointed with the Holy Ghost.[32] The cornerstone of the true Temple is Christ Himself.

With a broad consensus of the Fathers giving a sure interpretation for the *"ladder"* and the *"stone"*, we discover further divine touches in the details. Four times in this short passage the Scripture tells us Jacob slept. We are meant to notice the 'sleep'. We are told that this was *"after the setting of the sun"*, as with Abram (Gen 15:12), so we may think again of Christ, our spiritual Sun, descending into death, the light going out.

Four times here we hear of the מָקוֹם (place). A clue to what place we discern in reading: *"being afraid, Jacob said: 'How fearful this place is!'"* (Gen 28:17) Twice in this verse is Hebrew fear: יָרֵא (for *afraid, fearful*). The first ten times the Torah uses this word, each instance teaches about refining our relation to God. This יָרֵא is salutary, for it is that *"fear of the Lord [which] is the beginning of wisdom"* (Prov 9:10). Fear belongs to the *"place"*. While the *"place"* appeared like little more than a rocky desert, through healthy fear Jacob had his eyes and his mind opened, he was granted divine wisdom to see it as God's chosen place on earth.

---

[32] St Justin Martyr, *Dialogue with Trypho*, 86.

And what is God's chosen place on earth, the most important place to Him, other than where He came to dwell with men and to die for them? It was a fearful place but there a ladder rose to Heaven. So there are divine depths to the Crucifixion, which, when the dereliction was over, opened Heaven.

Examining the foundation for all this, Jerusalem's Temple Institute avows:

> Creation, all of it — its beginning and its conclusion — was all here, focused and concentrated in a simple rock, that just the night before had been many rocks, twelve, in fact, that *Yaakov* gathered beneath his head, and now were forged into one single rock that from this time forth would be known as the Foundation Stone, because in this simple, unimposing rock was the DNA of all creation.[33]

With the rabbis we may think of the twelve sons of Jacob who, after reconciliation, were to be made one. As Christians we think of the twelve Apostles who Christ made into one foundation for His Church.[34] St Peter exhorts all members of the Church to be *"living stones"* like Jesus, built up into the House of God:

> *be also yourselves like living stones, built upon [the Lord],*
> *a spiritual house, a holy priesthood, so as to offer up*
> *spiritual sacrifices, acceptable to God through Jesus Christ.*
> (1 Pet 2:5)

Like its foundation, the *"ladder"* was made of stone. In the Hebrew Bible the word is unique — סֻלָּם. In the Greek, the word

---

[33] The Temple Institute, *And he dreamed, and behold!* (Gen 28:12), Nov 2021.

[34] Even when Judas was chipped away, the 'twelve' remained, he being replaced with St Matthias.

κλίμαξ (climax) appears three times: once here, then twice in Nehemiah to describe the stone staircase *"descending"* and *"ascending"* to the City of David (Neh 3:15; 12:37). As the Son of God descended to ascend, so for us a descent into poverty, sickness, humiliation, captivity, or other tribulation can be, if willingly borne, an ascent spiritually.[35] When we accept our own crosses, then the angels descend to comfort us; when we assist at Holy Mass, the angels ascend raising our souls with them. In Latin the word used is *scala*.[36] We may think of a musical scale. So fifteen of the Psalms are sung under the title: *"A Song of Ascents"* (Ps 119-133). These refer to the steps of the Temple where the Levites took position to sing the Psalms for feasts and for the daily sacrifice. It represents the spiritual ascent we are to make, the growth in grace:

> *Blessed are they that dwell in thy house, O Lord: they shall praise thee for ever and ever. Blessed is the man whose help is from thee: in his heart he hath disposed to ascend by steps… For the lawgiver shall give a blessing, they shall go from virtue to virtue.* (Ps 83:5-7)

By dwelling in the House of the Lord we may ascend from virtue to virtue. The biological life which we inherited from Adam, but

---

[35] The ladder *"stands / leans"* (נִצָּב v.12) and likewise the Lord *"stands / leans"* (נִצָּב v.13) upon it. This is how the Lord appeared at Mamre to Abraham: *"three men, standing near him"* (Gen 18:2). God stands. This same is how Jacob later *"erected"* an altar (Gen 33:20) and *"set up"* a stone for a pillar (Gen 35:14). The altar stands. This is how Joseph's sheaf, representing Jesus, *"stood erect"* while the others worshipped his (Gen 37:7). Our Saviour stands. This is how God placed Moses to see Him like no other man had: *"Behold, there is a place with me, and you shall stand upon the rock"* (Ex 33:21). Our Mediator stands.

[36] *Scala* only appears here and in 1 Macc 5:30 (for wartime scaling ladders).

which will be lost in this *"vale of tears"*, we saw in Noah will not be cursed but blessed for those who revere the Cross. Abram's story shows us the beginning of the life of faith, and Jacob's story shows this is just the beginning, that it must reach from earth to Heaven, ascending from virtue to virtue, natural to supernatural, from faith to hope to charity. This divine life in us exceeds all the goods of the world, so that the least person in Heaven excels the greatest of men on earth:

> *Amen I say to you, among those born of women, there has arisen no one greater than John the Baptist. Yet the least in the kingdom of heaven is greater than he.* (Mt 11:11)

Consistently, Jacob is depicted as a principle of the multiplication of life. When he tended Laban's flocks, they multiplied exceedingly, no matter what was contrived against him. He became the father of twelve sons and a daughter. God changed his name to Israel, a name inherited by a whole people. Of course he points to Christ, and his twelve sons to the twelve Apostles, and the earthly foundation he rested upon with its vision of a ladder reaching Heaven points upward to the human-divine union in Jesus Who accomplishes that from all the tribes of Israel 'twelve times twelve times a thousand' are sealed for salvation: *"the number of those who were sealed: one hundred and forty-four thousand sealed, out of every tribe of the sons of Israel"* (Apoc 7:4). It is a figurative number of plentitude. Even beyond this St John saw:

> *a great crowd, which no one could number, from all the nations and tribes and peoples and languages, standing*

before the throne and in sight of the Lamb... And all the Angels were standing around the throne. (Apoc 7:11)

How can we join them? The place with the ladder reaching to Heaven is now everywhere, not only in the multiplication of altars in the churches around the world, but because literally everywhere we can receive the Cross — whether in suffering or in the Sacrament.

The Lord assured Jacob that He would not *"forsake"* him (עָזַב, ἐγκαταλείπω, *derelinquere* cf. Ps 22:1; Mt 27:46) until He *"accomplished all that I have said"* (Gen 28:15). On the Cross, Jesus kept this promise, fulfilling the Law, Prophets and Psalms to the letter, finally crying: *"It is accomplished"* (Jn 19:30 CJB).[37] As Jacob could see a foundation stone in an otherwise flat desert and declare it "the House of God" as if already built, so Jesus on laying the foundation of His Sacrifice could declare His work accomplished. He fulfilled what was written of Him in the OT, and thus He began a process so perfectly that it cannot be stopped until it is complete (cf. Jn 17:4; Phil 1:6). Purely by beginning the work of redemption of souls, He knew it would succeed through to the end of time, so that what was once a desert would end up as the fully inhabited House of God. No stone (or saint) is missing.

Finally, if the appearance of the ladder were in fact wooden rather than stone, this theme fits well with the Cross, as also does the flaming torch seen by Abraham (the light of Christ burning on the wood of the Cross) and the vineyard for Noah (intoxicating fruit hanging on wood). These motifs of wood point back to the Tree of Life, which became Adam's cross. What is this tree really? Jesus tells us that *"certainly a tree is known by its fruit"*

---

[37] CJB = Complete Jewish Bible by Dr. David H. Stern (1998).

(Mt 12:33). We will see later the fruit is the Body of Christ, and the Tree of Life is the Cross.

> *Christ has risen again from the dead, as the first-fruits of those who sleep... just as in Adam all die, so also in Christ all will be brought to life, but each one in his proper order: Christ, as the first-fruits... (1 Cor 15:20-23)*

AT THE CROSS
BEHOLD THY MOTHER

Jesus could have accomplished His work alone, but He chose a helper. Such is the pattern of salvation. Adam was given Eve. Noah would have saved no one but himself had he not had a wife. The promise to Abraham was fulfilled only in conjunction with Sarah. Alone Jacob would not have become multitudinous Israel. God too wants many children, but born in the spirit, that is who *"are born, not of blood, nor of the will of the flesh, nor of the will of man, but of God"* (Jn 1:13). It is fitting that these children also have a Mother, not of the flesh, but one fully receptive to the Will of God. So our Redeemer Jesus Christ was pleased to appoint a helper in His saving work, the Co-Redemptrix, Mary His Mother.

St John bears witness to this. Describing the day of the Crucifixion in his Gospel, five times St John writes the command: *"Behold"* (Jn 19:4,6,14,26,27). In regard to Jesus, Pilate announced to all of us: *"Behold Him… Behold the Man… Behold your King…"* After this Jesus said to His Mother Mary: *"Woman, behold your son"*, then He said to St John: *"Behold your mother*". This fivefold 'behold' is meant for all of us. We are to contemplate Jesus; understand He is true Man; and that He is our Lord; that God entrusts those whom He loves to Mary; and that Mary is our Mother.

We might recall there were three Marys who contemplated the Crucifixion (Jn 19:25). Mary of Cleophas, not yet believing, watched and bore witness. Mary Magdalene, not yet hoping, came and shed tears. Mary the Mother of God, full of faith, hope and charity, freely offered her Son for the salvation of the world. Her spiritual cooperation with God was perfect. Since Eden God had waited for this! Mary reversed the error of our first mother, paying a greater price than Eve. Because of original sin, God said the woman would suffer pain in childbirth (Gen 3:16). Mary had not suffered the slightest pain in giving birth to Jesus in Bethlehem, but her agony surrendering Him on Calvary felt like a myriad deaths.[38] It was in fact a myriad childbirths: in the transforming sacrifice, Our Lady became Mother of the Church.

This is not easy to discern from the NT alone. The OT helps us. In the following sections we will see how the experiences foreshadowing the Passion of Abimelech, Isaac and Boaz essentially involve Sarah, Rebekah and Ruth. Between them these women help show three supernatural relationships which began on Calvary: the Church's spiritual marriage to Christ, the Church as our Mother and the Virgin Mary as our Mother.

---

[38] Pope Alexander III (✝1181), *Letter to the Sultan of Iconium* "Mary conceived without shame, bore without pain." See also Is 66:7-8.

Abimelech's Enlightening Dream

Abraham said about his wife Sarah: 'She is my sister.' Therefore, Abimelech, the king of Gerar, sent for her and took her. Then God came to Abimelech through a dream in the night, and he said to him: 'Lo, you shall die because of the woman that you have taken. For she has a husband.' In truth, Abimelech had not touched her, and so he said: 'Lord, would you put to death a people, ignorant and just? Did he not say to me, "She is my sister," and did she not say, "He is my brother"? In the sincerity of my heart and the purity of my hands, I have done this.' And God said to him: 'And I know that you have acted with a sincere heart. And therefore I kept you from sinning against me, and I did not release you to touch her. Now therefore, return his wife to the man, for he is a prophet. And he will pray for you, and you will live. But if you are not willing to return her, know this: you shall die a death, you and all that is yours.' And immediately Abimelech, rising up in the night, called all his servants. And he spoke all these words in their hearing, and all the men were very afraid. Then Abimelech called also for Abraham, and he said to him: 'What have you done to us? How have we sinned against you, so that you would bring so great a sin upon me and upon my kingdom? You have done to us what you ought not to have done... What did you see, so that you would do this?' Abraham responded: 'I thought to myself, saying: Perhaps there is no fear of God in this place. And they will put me to death because of my wife. Yet, in another way, she is also truly my sister, the daughter of my father, and not the daughter of my mother, and I took her as a wife. Then, after God led me out of my father's house, I said to her: "You will show this mercy to me. In every place, to which we will travel, you will say that I am your brother."' Therefore, Abimelech took sheep and oxen, and men servants and women servants, and he gave them to Abraham. And he returned his wife Sarah to him. And he said, 'The land is in your sight. Dwell wherever it will please you.' Then to Sarah he said: 'Behold, I have given your brother one thousand silver coins. This will be for you as a veil for your eyes, to all who are with you and wherever you will travel. And so, remember that you were taken.' Then when Abraham prayed, God healed Abimelech and his wife, and his handmaids, and they gave birth. For the Lord had closed every womb of the house of Abimelech, because of Sarah, the wife of Abraham.

— Gen 20:2-18

Abimelech of Gerar, a Philistine king, was put to confusion by the relationship between Abraham and Sarah: were they sister and brother, or husband and wife? Although perplexed, he showed great reverence for marriage, and thereby paid remote honour to the related reality of God's union with man through the Church. Accordingly, God was favourable to him. We too, if we respect and abide by the natural law, will be well disposed to better understand the supernatural.

Thanks to a God-given *"dream in the night"*, Abimelech came to understand more fully Abraham's relationship with Sarah, namely that they were not merely (half-)siblings but were married. Abraham clarified that his wife was in a certain degree his sister:

in another way, she is also truly my sister, the daughter of my father, and not the daughter of my mother, and I took her as a wife. (Gen 20:8)

He had adopted the same cover story in Egypt with Pharaoh. A century later his son Isaac would do the same again here in Gerar with another King Abimelech (Gen 12:11-13; 20:11; 26:6-13). In total, the peculiar relation of sister-spouse and confusion thereover is related to us three times so that we take notice. Unconsciously for those involved at the time, a mystery is being revealed to those who ponder its meaning in Jesus Christ.

Abraham's multi-layered ties with Sarah mirror the relationship of Christ and the Church, who is to Him both Sister and Bride. So we hear in the Canticle of Canticles: *"An enclosed garden is my sister, my spouse"* (Cant 4:12). There is no incest here, but another allusion to the Church, beginning with the Virgin Mary. Precisely how this double-relationship describes our relation to Christ, we will examine shortly. But first we continue with the account from Genesis.

Given the mystery represented by Sarah, Abimelech did well to contain himself: *"In truth, Abimelech had not touched her"* (Gen 20:4). By character Abimelech had a genuine reverence for marriage, confessing the *"sincerity of my heart and the purity of my hands"* (Gen 20:5) and reckoning adultery would *"bring so great a sin upon me and upon my kingdom"* (Gen 20:9).

In reward for this natural virtue, God condescended to warn Abimelech in a dream that Abraham and Sarah had been joined in one flesh and no man should put them asunder. The whole of

Abimelech's civilisation was at stake. If the king did not respect this marriage, his people would die out:

> *if you are not willing to return her, know this: you shall die a death, you and all that is yours… For the Lord had closed every womb of the house of Abimelech, because of Sarah, the wife of Abraham.* (Gen 20:7,18)

The same is true of nations today whose governments embrace the culture of death. If they do not respect natural marriage, they die out. Where Abimelech did not *"touch"* (נָגַע) Sarah, the same word is used by Eve reporting God's command about fruit of the Tree of Life: *"You shall not eat from it or touch it lest you die"* (Gen 3:3). Abimelech, though *"ignorant and just"* (Gen 20:4), respected the Creator's order. By overcoming concupiscence, he was receptive to God, and therefore rewarded with life-giving understanding. Each monarch or people who, repenting like Abimelech of their ignorant attempt to subjugate the Church or ignore the natural law on marriage (the two errors go together), seeking instead to honour God's design, will be spared divine wrath. Thanks to the mediation of Jesus Christ, they will be granted life and fruitfulness.

Adopting another angle to seek the Passion in this story, may we take Abraham to represent the Divinity of Christ and Abimelech to represent His Humanity?[39] Nowhere in the chapter are we told Abraham slept, for the Divinity does not sleep, does not die. But we know Abimelech slept, as God enlightened him about Sarah during a dream in the night. Let this sleep stand for

---

[39] Abraham's name means: 'Father of many nations' — we are generated through Christ's Divinity. Abimelech's name means: 'My father is king' — honouring Christ in His Humanity, Who is our King by birthright and conquest.

the Passion of Christ, which Jesus suffered in His Humanity, not His Divinity.

With this key, hidden meaning is opened up in the verses which follow:

Abimelech, rising up in the night, called all his servants. And he spoke all these words in their hearing, and all the men were very afraid. (Gen 20:8)

After Jesus' Passion (Abimelech's sleep) comes the Resurrection (*"rising up in the night"*); followed by gathering His disciples (*"called all his servants"*); and opening their hearts by explaining to them to the mysteries God (*"spoke all these words in their hearing"*); so the disciples were filled with wisdom (*"all the men were very afraid"* — fear of the Lord being the beginning of wisdom).

The divine intervention in Abimelech's sleep was a revelation:

return his wife to the man, for he is a prophet. And he will pray for you, and you will live... [if not] you shall die a death, you and all that is yours. (Gen 20:7-8)

Abimelech had not touched Sarah, as Jesus did not cling to human companionship, but surrendered it all with His life in sacrifice to God. It follows allegorically: *"when Abraham prayed, God healed Abimelech and his wife, and his handmaids, and they gave birth"* (Gen 20:17). Abraham symbolises Jesus' Divinity, by the power of whose word Abimelech was healed — that is the Resurrection. Death had lost its sting. Had this not happened, it would not be Abimelech alone who died, but *"all that is yours".* In this context that means if Jesus our Head had not risen, then no one could enter Heaven.

Happily, the Resurrection of Jesus' Humanity was not for Him alone. Rather He came in order to bring an enormous harvest of souls to God, indeed to restore what would otherwise be lost. Hence we read:

> *Abimelech took sheep and oxen, and men servants and women servants, and he gave them to Abraham. And he returned his wife Sarah to him… [and gave] one thousand silver coins.* (Gen 20:14)

So God's People were not lost, but thanks to the Passion (Abimelech's dream), Christ restores them to God as Bride, more greatly multiplied and enriched after the Passion than before: the *"sheep and oxen"* represent the numerous flock of faithful; the *"men servants and women servants"* represent clerics and religious; the *"silver coins"* speak of imperishable graces. All this was won through the Passion of Christ.

Now we return to consider the double-relationship of the Church as both Christ's Sister and His Bride. What does this mean?

Abraham and Sarah had the same father but different mothers. He is her brother and her husband. Allegorically, Christ is our Brother in the flesh, because all human bodies are descended from Adam, thus we have a shared father. But our spirits do not come from our parents, they are created directly by God. And our espousal to Christ is spiritual, in which regard He and we have different 'mothers'. The Son's divine Spirit, to put it poetically, can issue only from the womb of eternity — *"ex utero ante luciferum genui te"* (Ps 109:3).[40] Meanwhile, our spirit was created in time, *ex nihilo*, from the womb of pure potential, our metaphysical 'mother'.

So our relation with Jesus Christ is as to a brother in biological descent, because our bodies come from one father, while our spiritual relation with Jesus is a kind of marriage (Eph 5:32), legitimate precisely because we are different in our spiritual origin. Because there is between His Spirit and ours a 'male-female complementarity' (here meaning Uncreated and created respectively), then a much more intimate union is conceivable: *"whoever is joined to the Lord is one spirit"* (1 Cor 6:17). His Spirit penetrates our spirits. In fact we are also One Flesh with Him, but not in any sexual congress, rather assimilated as members of His Body. Even this, as He told us, is not by carnal but by spiritual generation, in both Baptism and the Holy Eucharist (Jn 3:5-6; 6:64). St Paul writes: *"preserve the unity of the Spirit within the bonds of peace. One body and one Spirit: to this you have been called"* (Eph 4:3-4). The cells of the body do not overlap, they are like brother and sister. Meanwhile spirits which unite are distinct but not separate, truly they live within each other, more like husband and wife.

---

[40] Or less poetically, the Son of God is generated from a single principle, God the Father. The Holy Spirit proceeds from the Father and Son also as from a single principle. There is no duality, no other god to be mother. The Living God is fruitful in 'celibacy'.

Or we can say though God is the Father of us all (albeit differentially, as Jesus says: *"I am ascending to My Father and to your Father"* Jn 20:17), yet our mothers are not the same. Unlike Jesus, all of our mothers suffer from original sin. Only Jesus was born to a mother without original sin, the Blessed Virgin Mary, immaculately conceived. The *Theotokos* is a different kind of mother.

Matrimony is an apt allegory for our union with God. Origen makes striking parallels between marriage and divine—human communion in teaching "the appellations of Bride and Bridegroom denote either the Church in her relation to Christ, or the soul in her union with the Word of God".[41] He continues that it is as if God kisses us when we allow our mind to be infused with deeper understanding of Him:

> And let us understand that by the 'mouth' of the Bridegroom is meant the power by which He enlightens the mind and, as by some word of love addressed to her — if so she deserve to experience the presence of power so great — makes plain whatever is unknown and dark to her. And this is the truer, closer, holier kiss, which is said to be granted by the Bridegroom-Word of God to the Bride — that is to say, to the pure and perfect soul; it is of this happening that the kiss, which we give one to another in church at the holy mysteries, is a figure.

However ardently two lovers wish to kiss, much stronger is God's desire to join His mouth to ours, to breathe His Spirit into ours. This love is not carnal but purer than light. Still the carnal image is good because most of us have an idea of how powerful passion can be; it gives us pause to think God's love for us is infinitely stronger than our love for anyone. When suddenly we do understand something of God that we did not see a moment before, or when we are inflamed with sudden devotion for Him, the cause might well be that God just kissed our soul. Indeed this

---

[41] Origen, *Commentary on the Canticle of Canticles,* 1.

union is so much more intimate than marriage that even one so articulate as St Augustine struggled to describe it:

> It is obscure and hard to understand how the human soul and the Word of God are united or mingled, or whatever word may be used to express this connection between God and the creature. It is from this connection that Christ and the Church are called Bridegroom and Bride, or husband and wife.[42]

Marriage is the highest natural good, the crowning of Creation. It is everywhere. It is given by God to teach us about the highest supernatural good: union with God. The similarities between marriage and union with God are instructive and so are the differences. The similarities point to obvious goods: new life, companionship, devotion. The differences too are vital. Love with God is not libidinous but much better and while the bond of a sacramental marriage dissolves upon death, the total penetration of a soul by the divine is made for eternity.[43] The archetype of marriage is the Incarnation. In Jesus the eternal *Logos* was perfectly united with a created human soul. This is the seed of the nuptial union of Jesus Christ with the Church, the Bridegroom with the Bride, the Creator with the creature.

Creation is ordered precisely to reveal the supernatural order. What is difficult for us to understand — the invisible, the distant, the divine — is indicated by what is easier for us to understand — the visible, close to us, material. To say "grace builds on nature"

---

[42] St Augustine, *Contra Faustum*, XXII, 40. See also 38.

[43] St Augustine, *Contra Faustum*, XIV, 3 "...you [the Church] know well that the gift which you desire from your Bridegroom is eternal life, for He Himself is eternal life."

means that whatever in human activity accords with the natural law, that is with right reason, is a perfect basis into which grace can be infused. This layered correspondence is taught by St Paul: *"For the husband is the head of the wife, just as Christ is the head of the Church"* (Eph 5:23). Society would be much more accepting of the first part if we pondered the goodness of the second. Reciprocally, this is made apparent when husbands love their wives as Christ did the Church, giving Himself entirely for her. Marriage is a high work.

In summary, by looking upon Jesus Christ we see a Man, our Brother. But invisibly, if we are baptised, then we are in a nuptial communion with His Divinity: *"For your Maker is your husband, the Lord of hosts is his name"* (Is 54:5 RSVCE). It was on Calvary that Our Lord proposed to the Church. It was on Calvary that Our Lady ratified the Church's "yes". Abraham and Sarah outline this mystery: Brother and Husband; Sister and Bride. In the next section we see that the bridal relationship develops to motherhood.

ISAAC SLEEPS WITH REBEKAH

*And he had gone out to meditate in the field, as daylight
was now declining. And when he had lifted up his eyes, he
saw camels advancing from afar. Likewise, Rebekah, having
seen Isaac, descended from the camel. And she said to the
servant, 'Who is that man who advances to meet us through
the field?' And he said to her, 'That is my lord.' And so,
quickly taking up her cloak, she covered herself... And
Isaac led her into the tent of Sarah his mother, and he
accepted her as wife. And he loved her so very much, that it
tempered the sorrow which befell him at his mother's death.*

— Gen 24:63-67

When Isaac ascended Mount Moriah, and was bound there by
Abraham to be sacrificed, he distinctly prefigured Jesus Christ
(Gen 22). As Jesus carried His Cross, so Isaac carried the wood
for his own holocaust up the same great rock where 1,800 years
later Jesus was crucified. Isaac survived, a ram crowned with
thorns being offered in his place.[44] Many years later, Isaac would
return to that place and complete his foreshadowing of Christ's
work on Calvary, not indeed by dying, but by offering new life.
While, visibly, the Crucifixion was a bloody death, it was then

---

[44] St Bede, *A Biblical Miscellany, On Tobias*, 6. Translated by W. Trent Foley
(LUP, 1999) "a ram aptly signifies Christ's humanity and a human being His
divinity..." "one reads in the expositions of the fathers that this single person
of the mediator [Jesus] who suffers to save the world is represented both by
Isaac, whose father offered him on the altar, and by the ram that was slain. That
person in His humanity was slaughtered like a sheep, yet in His divinity
remains immune to suffering along with God Father, even as Isaac returned
home alive along with his own father."

that invisibly, in the heart of Mary, Holy Mother Church took her beginnings. So Isaac returned to the place and met Rebekah who, when they were hidden from the eyes of the world, there consented to become mother of his children.

Sacred Scripture stresses that Isaac and Abraham went *"together"* (יַחְדָּו Gen 22:6,8; cf.19) to the *Akeidah* (Isaac's binding), suggesting they were united in heart. Isaac trusted in his father even during their great test. But some Midrashim say when his mother Sarah found out, she was so confounded by the shock of nearly losing her beloved, only-begotten son, promised by God, and at the hands of her husband, that she separated from Abraham.[45] He dwelt in Beersheba (Gen 22:19); Sarah spent her last days in Hebron and died (Gen 23:2).

The loss of his mother was a deep blow for Isaac. His father sent a steward to find a wife for him. Journeying north to meet this future wife, Isaac paused at the place of his binding.[46] Understandably, in this place, Isaac was wistful, contemplative: *"he had gone out to meditate in the field"* (Gen 24:63). The word for *"meditate"* (שׂוּחַ), is used only here in the Bible. This is fitting, for Isaac's thoughts must have been unique: remembering how at his binding he freely offered himself for immolation at the hands of his own father, and returning to the place now he could willingly put his mother's death into God's Hands too. Who else

---

[45] If this is true, it highlights how perfect are the faith and love of the Virgin Mary who did not hold back her Son.

[46] Though not explicit in the Torah, solid traditions relate that Isaac first met Rebekah in the same place where he had almost been immolated as a sacrifice. This is plausible given Rebekah did not delay (Gen 24:55-59) and Isaac stopped to *"meditate"* (Gen 24:63). As God organised the success of the mission to find Rebekah (Gen 24:42-51), it is a small thing for Him to fix also the location for their first encounter at the most meaningful place on the planet.

but Jesus could understand this double work of Isaac's soul? Mystically in Christ, Isaac experienced a deep part in the Passion.

From the Cross Jesus looked up to Heaven at the ninth hour knowing soon He would win His Spouse. Here Isaac *"as the daylight was now declining... lifted up his eyes"* (Gen 24:63) and saw from afar his bride-to-be. The phrase *"lifted up his eyes"* typically refers to worship.[47] We should bear this connotation in mind. Meanwhile she, Rebekah, *"an exceedingly elegant girl, and a most beautiful virgin, and unknown by man"* (Gen 24:16) saw him and heard, *"That is my lord* [κύριός]*"* (Gen 24:65). The two went into the tent and became one flesh. Isaac was comforted over the death of his mother because there with Rebekah he entered matrimony, which means 'to make a mother'. They slept. They woke. So life continues despite death.

Forgive me for another recap, but these stories are so simply written, and the truths buried in them so profound, that we need to read them many times for the light to dawn. Aged about thirty, Isaac had prefigured the beginning of Christ's work on Calvary, ascending the mountain and being lain on the wood, and survived. After losing and mourning his mother, Isaac then consummated his prefiguration of Calvary, not in death, but in love. Given Rebekah is a type of the Blessed Virgin Mary (see Gen 24 for her goodness, and Gen 27 for her practical wisdom), could the union in the flesh of Isaac and Rebekah at the very place of his binding prefigure that union in the spirit of the Son of God with Our Lady at the Crucifixion? At the Cross, Mary was made a mother — *"Ecce mater tua"* (Jn 19:27) — and Our Lord cried, *"It is consummated"* (Jn 19:30).

---

[47] In the worst case it indicates paying homage to idols. See Ezek 33:25.

We might say that as Isaac in making a new mother in marriage (Rebekah) was consoled regarding the death of his biological mother (Sarah), so Jesus, although sorrowing on Calvary for Mary, pained by her grievous sorrows, was consoled in making her Mother of all God's children. The natural sorrow at the death of her Son was superseded by the joy at what would come in the supernatural order: Jesus risen in glory and billions of children to follow. Or else we can think of the synagogue as Jesus' mother, whom on Calvary He lost, but in His Blood He sealed a New Covenant making the Church a Mother most fruitful.

In either case, the Torah speaks of Jesus by its description of Isaac: *"And he loved her so very much, that it tempered the sorrow which befell him at his mother's death"* (Gen 24:67). This may mean Jesus was so pleased by the glory that would be awarded to Mary for her work with Him (because He *"loved her so very much"*) that this tempered the thought of the sorrow inflicted on her on Calvary, her spiritual martyrdom. Mary was both Sarah and Rebekah, both the Mother who died and the Mother would give new life. Or in the second interpretation, Jesus could bear the passing of the Old Covenant given its fulfilment the New, that is, *mutatis mutandis*, the mother had died but the bride had arrived.

Isaac loved his mother Sarah so much that after she died it seems he took her tent with him on his journeys. We read: *"he led [Rebekah] into the tent of Sarah his mother, and he accepted her as wife"* (Gen 24:67). Isaac dwelling in Sarah's tent may signify Jesus being at home in the Old Covenant, for He loved the Law. He wrote it! But concealed deep within the Old Covenant is the New. A *"tent"* (אֹהֶל, Ex 26:7) is what Moses was instructed to fashion to cover the *"tabernacle"* (מִשְׁכָּן), in which the brand-new ark of the covenant was contained, forming layers of truth. And it was from within Sarah's tent that a new union was formed and, in due course, new life would emerge.[48] While Isaac's binding took place in the open air, the union he formed there with Rebekah was hidden from the eyes of the world. So Jesus' Crucifixion was public, but the fruit of it was invisible, supernatural, a union of His Sacred Heart with Mary's Immaculate Heart.

To illustrate that a biological relationship can image a spiritual relationship, or that a personal relationship can represent a universal one (for example Mary as Mother of the Church), it might help here to take a diversion into distinguishing three levels of maternity and paternity: biological, natural and supernatural.[49] First there is biological generation. At this level there is an obvious difference between the male and the female. A man can generate children biologically every day, with a potential for thousands of offspring. A woman can conceive for only a minority of days in the month, and then cannot conceive again until after the pregnancy is over. Evidently there is an irreducible difference between males and females. This difference is analogously present in paternity and maternity at the natural and supernatural levels also.

Natural paternity is the father's duty in raising a child: providing for mother and child, protecting them both, teaching the child skills, disciplining and playing with the child, demonstrably loving their mother. Beside bodily and psychological goods, and

---

[48] Some twenty verses later, we read Rebekah miraculously conceived (Gen 25:21). Their son Jacob also loved to dwell in tents.

[49] For an analysis of this topic, see Carter Griffin, *Supernatural Fatherhood through Priestly Celibacy* (2011).

beyond education, the highest part of natural paternity is to teach virtues, especially by example. Evidently a man can reach even more people in natural paternity than biological paternity. A dedicated man, whether he has biological children or not, can provide food and shelter for scores of orphans, he can discipline hundreds, educate thousands, inspire millions. He may not neglect his own to do this, but as fatherhood essentially involves perfecting the form of others by giving of oneself, then the more manly a man is, to all the more can he serve as father. Necessarily while one can have only one biological father, one can have many natural fathers, very many who contribute to one's formation.

Natural maternity is receptive of another. Both mother and father should listen to their children (and to each other), but a mother is generally more gifted at understanding what someone is saying even when they do not speak. Perception is receptive. Both mother and father hold their baby and embrace their child, but in its deepest pain a child normally runs to its mother. Indeed part of the father's task is to teach the child to be independent, to be able to separate itself emotionally from its mother. No one will say natural motherhood is not active in a thousand ways, but its genius is in receiving and in giving attention to individuals rather than directing the masses (or armies, populations, workforces).

Then supernatural paternity, or spiritual paternity, is anything we do actively to provide a soul with graces. On the biological level, the male gamete fertilises the female gamete and God inspires a newly created soul. Analogously, in supernatural paternity one person acts, another soul receives, and God infuses the grace. Such actions include: to take a baby to be baptised, to take a child to Holy Mass, to read the Bible to someone, to pray the Holy Rosary for (or with) them, to catechise, to give an icon, to assist someone with First Holy Communion or Confirmation classes. Obviously both men and woman can do all this. However, a man who becomes a priest enjoys greatly multiplied opportunities for giving the Sacraments, for preaching, for catechising, for providing pastoral assistance. If he has had a good formation, then the form he will pass on is high indeed. Masculinity will show itself in orderly liturgy, in fearless preaching, in clear catechising, in pastoral devotion. Holy bishops discipline their clerical sons, much more interested in justice than popularity. And how many souls can be reached in spiritual fatherhood? Two thousand years ago St Paul wrote:

For you might have ten thousand instructors in Christ, but not so many fathers. For in Christ Jesus, through the Gospel, I have begotten you. (1 Cor 4:15)

Given that just about every Christian alive benefits from the letters of St Paul, it means he is still forming spiritual children today, at least as an instructor if not a begetter. The fruitfulness is incalculable. Yet there is a way for human beings to be more fruitful still: supernatural maternity. Once again, for understanding, we turn to Mary.

For God to give His most to the world, there had to be a person who would receive Him in full. And that was Mary, His Mother. Her qualification for this was purity of body and soul — her flesh, her emotions, her mind, her will — which meant there was no impediment or diminution whatsoever in her reception of all that God offered. He became incarnate in her. Our Lady is true biological mother to Jesus; and perfect natural mother to Him and doubtless to some others round about; and most sublime spiritual mother to literally all God's children. This is not primarily achieved in any act of Mary's but in her suffering. Perhaps, then, we can say: if spiritual paternity involves an action by man through which, if it corresponds to His Will, God sends grace to others, then spiritual maternity is passive, it is suffering, it is lovingly accepting a sacrifice for the sake of the Father. This moves the Father to act, to send grace. And of all creatures Mary, being immaculately conceived, was able to receive the most, and Mary suffered the most, and accepted willingly the highest possible sacrifice — her dear Son dying on the Cross. And for this the Unmoved Mover was moved to make her Mother of all. To understand that Jesus was comforted on Calvary, even joyful in spirit, we may meditate on Isaac being comforted in that same place by Rebekah.

Rebekah is an impressive figure in Genesis, winning our hearts. With Sarah and Rachel, she helps us better understand Our Lady. Reciprocally, Our Lady dresses the OT Matriarchs with glory, completing the high purpose of their lives. In the Old the New is concealed, and in the New the Old is revealed.

BOAZ'S MIDNIGHT COMPANION

She answered: Whatsoever thou shalt command, I will do. And she went down to the [threshing floor], and did all that her mother-in-law had bid her. And when Booz had eaten, and drunk, and was merry, he went to sleep by the heap of sheaves, and she came softly and uncovering his feet, laid herself down. And behold, when it was [the middle of the night] the man was afraid, and troubled: and he saw a woman lying at his feet. And he said to her: Who art thou? And she answered: I am Ruth thy handmaid: spread thy coverlet over thy servant, for thou art a near kinsman. And he said: Blessed art thou of the Lord, my daughter, and thy latter kindness has surpassed the former: because thou hast not followed young men either poor or rich. Fear not therefore, but whatsoever thou shalt say to me I will do to thee. For all the people that dwell within the gates of my city, know that thou art a virtuous woman.

— Rth 3:5-11 (DRB)

The six foregoing prefigurations of the Passion of Christ were all from the Book of Genesis. In the first, the theme of sleep (Adam's) is absolutely central, and the involvement of a woman (Eve) likewise crucial. In the cases following this, the theme of sleep is sometimes explicit (Noah, Abram, Jacob) and sometimes inferred (Abimelech, Isaac). The association of a woman is sometimes intimate (as with Isaac) or indirect (for Abimelech), and sometimes remote (for Noah, Abram, Jacob). In the next case, from the Book of Ruth, both the sleep and the role of the woman are essential to the prefiguration.

Perhaps God wants to make it more obvious to us, because He does not want us to miss it as we read through the OT. Decoded by Christ, the Book of Ruth as a whole offers the reader comforting insight into how good-natured is our heavenly Mother Mary and assures us of her assiduous care. Here we will concentrate on the foreshadowing of her mystical sacrifice.

Powerful Boaz, great grandfather of King David and progenitor of Jesus Christ, eats, drinks, and falls asleep, somewhat merry in wine. The beautiful Ruth, washed and anointed, goes to the threshing floor and lies at Boaz's feet, and there the two of them sleep, covered by one mantel. What does this mean, this woman so humble and submissive at his feet, honouring him, adoring him? Without any shadow of doubt this is about the Blessed Virgin Mary, Co-redemptrix, suffering martyrdom on Calvary with Christ her Son.

Jesus is prefigured when we read: *"This Boaz... this night he will winnow the threshing floor"* (Rth 3:2). St John the Baptist announced of Jesus: *"He will purify His threshing floor. And He will gather the wheat into the barn. But the chaff He will burn with unquenchable fire"* (Lk 3:17). Calvary is the threshing floor. Jesus' Sacrifice on the Cross began by separating the Good Thief from the Bad, the first to Paradise, the other to the everlasting fire. Then, advancing through time, His Sacrifice represented in Holy Mass dissolves whole empires *"like the chaff of a summer's threshing floor"* while the Risen Jesus becomes *"a great mountain [filling] the whole earth"* (Dan 2:35 DRB). So the Mass, Mount Calvary, is everywhere. Woe to those peoples who reject it. The Prophet Micah declares that the peoples do not understand why they are being drawn to Mount Sion, the Church, but there God will shatter them *"together like hay on a threshing floor"* (Mic 4:12). It is in our response to the Cross — to Holy Mass, to the Holy Eucharist — that the issue is decided, souls are sorted: wheat or chaff, destined respectively for the barn or the fire.

Sleeping *"by the heap of sheaves"* (Rth 3:7 DRB) gives a Eucharistic accompaniment, as does the drinking of wine. We are told that Boaz *"finished eating and drinking"* (Rth 3:7), which sets the scene for what followed the Last Supper, where Jesus, significantly, finished eating and drinking. Boaz being pleasantly tipsy in his sleep is a gentle recollection of the more severe inebriations of Noah and Lot (Gen 9:21; 19:33). Yet in the middle of the night Boaz *"was afraid, and troubled"*. So we have too that mysterious tone which descended on Abraham (Gen 15:12).

For her part, Ruth's humility is seen in her saying: *"Whatsoever thou shalt command, I will do"* (Rth 3:5 DRB). She approaches Boaz *"softly"* (לַט), which word means 'secretly' or 'mysteriously', ultimately suggesting supernaturally, by grace. Later she calls herself Boaz's *"handmaid"* — as the Virgin Mary confessed herself *"handmaid of the Lord"* ready to do all as instructed (Lk 1:38). He in turn tells her *"Fear not"*, as Jesus was wont to say.

Ruth lying at Boaz's feet stands for Mary's compassionate presence at the foot of the Cross. Every word of the dialogue between Boaz and Ruth is the silent conversation of Jesus and Mary fulfilled on Calvary. That both Boaz and Ruth slept under one cloak means both Jesus and Mary suffered the Passion. So the Church honours Mary with the title Queen of Martyrs, St Bernard preaching: "Mary was a martyr, not by the sword of the executioner, but by bitter sorrow of heart", upon which words St Alphonsus comments:

If her body were not wounded by the hand of the executioner, her blessed heart was transfixed by a sword of grief at the Passion of her Son; grief which was sufficient to have caused her death, not once, but a thousand times. From this we shall see that Mary was not only a real martyr, but that her martyrdom surpassed all others; for it was longer than that of all others, and her whole life may be said to have been a prolonged death.[50]

The passage at the head of this section began with Ruth saying to her Jewish mother-in-law, *"Whatsoever thou shalt command, I will do"* (Rth 3:5 DRB); so the Virgin Mary is obedient to Jewish tradition. It ends with Boaz honouring Ruth as Jesus honours Mary:

> *whatsoever thou shalt say to me I will do to thee. For all the people that dwell within the gates of my city, know that thou art a virtuous woman.* (Rth 3:11 DRB)

That is, when those who dwell in the City of God beg for Our Lady's intercession, it is guaranteed to be effective since the Lord refuses her nothing.[51] And this is fitting as a little later we read: *"So she slept at his feet till the night was going off"* (Rth 3:14 DRB), meaning Mary participates in the Crucifixion until evil is ended. In return, Boaz fills her mantle with barley (Rth 3:15), while the Church sees the souls of the saved as gathered under Mary's mantle.

---

[50] St Alphonsus Ligouri, *Discourse IX of The Dolors Of Mary.*

[51] Pope Benedict XVI, *Address*, Etzelsbach, 23rd Sep 2011: "When Christians of all times and places turn to Mary, they are acting on the spontaneous conviction that Jesus cannot refuse His mother what she asks; and they are relying on the unshakable trust that Mary is also *our* mother..."

Ruth ensures her mother-in-law's family does not die out childless. Allegorically, thanks to the Virgin Mary, the Old Covenant did not end fruitless (cf. Rth 4:10,14), rather through her Son it was translated into the New. In biological reality, from Boaz and Ruth's union issued, ultimately, Jesus Christ.[52] Then from Jesus and Mary's spiritual collaboration issued, ultimately, all the children of God.

As mentioned, all this happened at Boaz's *"threshing floor"* (גֹּרֶן, ἅλων Rth 3:2,3,6). Threshing floors have deep links with the Crucifixion. It was at Araunah's *"threshing floor"* that *"the Angel of the Lord had extended his hand over Jerusalem, so that he might destroy it"* (2 Sam 24:16). But while the slaughter was underway, God ordered the angel to desist, having been appeased by King David's willingness to carry the whole punishment in order to spare his people (2 Sam 24:17). So Jesus.

Here on this threshing floor, fulfilling the words of the prophet, *"David built an altar to the Lord. And he offered holocausts and peace offerings"* (2 Sam 24:19-25). For the holocaust Aranauh supplied oxen and wood — we may think of flesh on the Cross — *"a king to a king"*, like Jesus to His Father. David insisted on giving payment, vowing: *"I will not offer to the Lord, my God, holocausts that cost nothing"* (2 Sam 24:23-24). So did Jesus, fulfilling the words (and lives) of the prophets, pay the price for our sins. God did not make His Sacrifice for free.[53]

---

[52] Jesus Christ, *"was descended from David according to the flesh"* (Rom 1:3). While St Joseph was certainly of the House of David (see Lk 2:4; 3:23,31), Jesus' biological descent is through His Mother, "a Virgin of the kingly lineage of David" (Pope St Leo the Great, *Sermon on the Feast of the Nativity*, I).

[53] At another *"threshing floor"* the twelve sons of Israel vehemently lamented the death of their father (Gen 50:10). So St John, representing the twelve Apostles, under the Cross acutely lamented the death of his Lord.

The Annunciation of the Blessed Virgin Mary had been prefigured by the woollen fleece at Gideon's *"threshing floor"* (Jdg 6:37). God's protection of Our Lady is indicated by Uzzah being suddenly *"divided"*, killed, for improperly touching the ark of the covenant at Chidon's *"threshing floor"* (1 Chron 13:9-11). The Assumption of Our Lady is prefigured by the ark of the covenant being brought with all solemnity to the House of God, to dwell in the Holy of Holies, across from the altar of holocaust (1 Kngs 6:8), built meaningfully at Araunah's *"threshing floor"* (1 Chron 21:28-22:1). So it had long been laid down by God that Mary would be present on Calvary for the holocaust of her Son, for the winnowing of souls, for the destiny of nations, for the final determination of the entire course of history.

Meanwhile, there is something so peaceful about Ruth's manner and her sleep that we may overlook that at *"midnight the man was afraid, and troubled"* (Rth 3:8 DRB). This is written because it denoted the two most terrible days in the world: the day of the Crucifixion, and the day of Judgement. The more we think about these two days, the more sense it makes that we cultivate a relationship with Our heavenly Mother. Praying, reading, making offerings to her honour, sacrifices for her intentions, will draw us to her. Otherwise it is hard to get to know the Mother of God. Not everyone's testimony is to be trusted, and we can easily deceive ourselves. The NT does not seem to say much about Mary (although in fact it speaks volumes). So God is pleased to give us aid through the OT. How valuable is the Book of Ruth!

THE CROSS IS OUR
BATTLE STANDARD

in hoc signo vinces

T he Cross is our standard, for *"The life of man upon earth is a warfare"* (Job 7:1). Keeping the Cross in mind orientates us on the battlefield, enabling ordered ranks before engagement, and our only hope of united action once the raging chaos of war surrounds us. This means we must learn to recognise and conform to the Cross already in times of ease if we are to withstand the onslaught of evil when it floods into our life. OT prefigurations demonstrate that through the Cross good will most certainly prevail and evil never had a chance. This is true in the cosmic struggle between good and evil, as well as the world historical struggle between the same, and, for all who cleave to the Cross, the struggle within the individual soul.

Five accounts are examined below. Moses shows good prevails by the power of the Cross while Samson shows evil is wiped out by the power of the Cross. Jonah shows this fight is against sin, death and hell, we cannot avoid it, and Jesus cannot lose. David shows the power of the Cross operates through self-sacrifice and with Saul he shows it demands mercy.

Perhaps we think we know all these truths anyway? But the OT stories give us vivid data in order that when evil hits us — which it will — we have an unshakeable foundation on which to stand. This fight is so much bigger than us. It is on a cosmic scale. We can learn by painful experience or else be well trained and forearmed through the Bible. The experiences of Moses, Jonah and David help us understand the content of NT revelation, which tells us God's Plan involves the Cross. It pleases the Father:

> *Through [Jesus] to reconcile all things unto Himself, making peace through the Blood of His Cross, both the things that are on earth and the things that are in heaven.* (Col 1:20 DRB)

Against such a high work, we should not doubt there exist enemies of the Cross, however futile their campaigns:

> *For many persons, about whom I have often told you (and now tell you, weeping) are walking as enemies of the Cross of Christ. Their end is destruction… for they are immersed in earthly things.* (Phil 3:18-19)

How shall we fight these? With the love Jesus showed on Calvary, *"making peace… [to] reconcile both to God in one body by the Cross, killing the enmities in Himself"* (Eph 2:15-16 DRB). His means are not worldly but supernatural:

so that you may be able to stand against the treachery of the devil. For our struggle is not against flesh and blood, but against principalities and powers, against the directors of this world of darkness, against the spirits of wickedness in high places. (Eph 6:11-12)

If our enemies are invisible, how shall we know how to overcome them? By gazing upon, and imitating, and wearing the Sign of the Cross. Being marked by it is the only way to survive the coming conflagration (Ezek 9:4-6; Apoc 7:3; 9:4; 14:1).

MOSES' WEARY ARMS OUTSTRETCHED

And Moses said to Joshua: 'Choose men. And when you go out, fight against Amalek. Tomorrow, I will stand at the top of the hill, holding the staff of God in my hand.' Joshua did as Moses had spoken, and he fought against Amalek. But Moses and Aaron and Hur ascended to the top of the hill. And when Moses lifted up his hands, Israel prevailed. But when he released them a little while, Amalek overcame. Then the hands of Moses became heavy. And so, taking a stone, they placed it beneath him, and he sat on it. Then Aaron and Hur sustained his hands from both sides. And it happened that his hands did not tire until the setting of the sun. And Joshua put to flight Amalek and his people by the edge of the sword. Then the Lord said to Moses: 'Write this, as a memorial in a book, and deliver it to the ears of Joshua. For I will wipe away the memory of Amalek from under heaven.' And Moses built an altar. And he called its name, 'The Lord, my Exaltation.' For he said: 'The hand of the throne of the Lord, and the war of the Lord, will be against Amalek from generation to generation.'

— Ex 17:8-16

No one in the OT is more like to Jesus than Moses (Dt 18:15,19; Acts 3:22; 7:37). The chief reason is that *"Moses was a man exceedingly meek, beyond all the men who were living upon the earth"* (Num 12:3). This word עָנָו, πραΰς means "meek" with connotations also of poverty and affliction.[54] So it is supremely apt for Jesus Who emptied Himself of His Divine riches to be afflicted upon the Cross. Imitating in advance Jesus Who decreed: *"anyone who will have spoken a word against the Son of man shall be forgiven"* (Mt 12:32), and from the Cross: *"Father, forgive them. For they know not what they do"* (Lk 23:34), Moses is forbearing enough to forgive those who have opposed him (Num 11:29; 12:13).[55] It is this meekness of Moses that makes him effective as mediator.[56] His ardour for his people was so strong that he could not bear to live if they were lost, praying most sincerely to the Lord:

> *I beg you, this people has sinned the greatest sin, and they have made for themselves gods of gold. Either release them from this offence, or, if you do not, then delete me from the book that you have written.* (Ex 32:30-32)

---

[54] After centuries of loving reflection on Moses, the greatest of all Hebrews, a short digest tells us the prevailing reason for his election: *"[God] made him holy by his faith and meekness* (πραΰτητι)*, and he chose him from among all flesh"* (Sir 45:4). As Jesus once said: *"Learn from Me, for I am meek* (πραΰς) *and humble of heart"* (Mt 11:29).

[55] St Augustine, *Enarration on Psalm 138* "In the time even of the Old Testament, when the carnal people was restrained by visible punishments, how did Moses, the servant of God, who by understanding belonged to the New Testament, how did he hate sinners when he prayed for them, or how did he not hate them when he slew them, save that he *'hated them with a perfect hatred'* (Ps 138:22)? For with such perfection did he hate the iniquity which he punished, as to love the manhood for which he prayed."

[56] *"'Forgive, I beseech you, the sins of this people, according to the greatness of your mercy, as you have been merciful to them from their going out of Egypt unto this place.' And the Lord said: 'I have forgiven according to your word'"* (Num 14:19-20; cf. Ex 32:11-14).

The love of Moses means more to God than all the sins of the Hebrews. That is staggering. The love of Jesus means more to God than all the sins of the world.

Unsurprisingly then we find in Moses' life a clear prefiguration of Jesus' Passion, not to speak of the many invisible sacrifices in the soul of this most meek man. Moses stretching out his arms in prayer while Joshua battled against Amalek is recognised by multiple Church Fathers as a figure of the Crucifixion.[57] St Justin Martyr taught that the battle was won because Moses made the sign of the Cross while praying, which was so pleasing to God that He could not but respond favourably to Moses' prayer. In combination with this, and crucially, one stronger than Moses was doing the fighting, namely Joshua, that is Yeshua (יְהוֹשׁוּעַ), meaning 'The Lord is Salvation', the Hebrew for Jesus. We will see how both Moses and Joshua prefigure Jesus in this example.

Moses' exertion approached exhaustion. To extend ones arms for the duration of a Rosary brings on aches if not pain. To maintain this posture all day is torture (even without being nailed to a cross). Battling the resultant tiredness, Moses' companions Aaron and Hur held up his arms. Thus like Jesus weary on Calvary, he is crucified between two others. This consuming fatigue is our connection with sleep, enough to make us explore whether Moses' exhaustion points to Jesus' 'sleep' on the Cross.

God is a Poet Who finds endless ways to allude to the way of our redemption and He expressly wanted these events written down: *"the Lord said to Moses: 'Write this, as a memorial in a book, and deliver it to the ears of Joshua'"* (Ex 17:14). Ever

---

[57] St Justin Martyr, *Dialogue with Trypho*, 90; St Gregory Nazianzus, *Oratio Secunda*, 88; St Gregory of Nyssa, *Life of Moses*, II, 78; St Augustine, *De Trinitate*, IV, 15, 20.

since, it has given Jews who read it comfort and strength. But for Christians, when once we see the Cross in the midst of it, it takes our breath away.

Did the Fathers say this event figures the Crucifixion because such an interpretation is possible to read into the text? Or is it that such an interpretation can be read into the text because God arranged it so, and 1,400 years later unlocked its meaning to His disciples? Certainly the second. And as God wanted it written down in the first place, would He not also come to explain it? Jesus Himself taught that Moses' bronze serpent in the desert figured His Crucifixion (Jn 3:14; Num 21:9). Why not also Moses' prayer on the hill with his arms stretched out, *"holding the staff of God in my hand"* (Ex 17:9), signifying the wood of the Cross? So he stood until vespers, or *"until the setting of the sun"* (Ex 17:12), a motif we recall from the stories of Abram and Jacob to signify the darkness which fell when Christ, our Sun, descended. Jesus is undoubtedly present here, working in Moses while Moses participates in Him.

If Moses is Christ on the Cross, what was Joshua's role? Is he not Jesus present and living in the souls of the baptised, commanding and strengthening the whole Christian army? For the battle was waged the whole day long, even *"until the setting of the sun"* (Ex 17:12). This represents the whole course of history. Moses being up on the mountain is not only a snapshot of Mount Calvary, but stands for the Crucifixion's place in the middle of time, or above time, outside of time. It is visible from the whole battlefield, as our redemption was promised from the beginning (Gen 3:15), so all can anticipate it or remember it. The strategy was made the day before the battle, Moses saying: *"Tomorrow, I will stand at the top of the hill..."* (Ex 17:9) This indicates God knew of Calvary from before the day of creation began. In such an interpretation, Moses represents Jesus our Eternal High Priest on high up in Heaven interceding ceaselessly for His Church, while simultaneously Joshua, who we are told has God's Spirit (Num 27:18; Dt 34:9), is Christ active within and among the baptised here below. Jesus promised *"I will not leave you orphans"* (Jn 14:18) but *"behold I am with you all days, even to the consummation of the world"* (Mt 28:20 DRB). We have no grounds for fear! It is impossible that evil should finally prevail against love. Jesus is with us, in our hearts and on our altars.

What is the significance of Aaron and Hur? Upholding Moses' right hand Aaron represents the pope and upholding the left hand Hur represents the king; or the priesthood and the secular powers; the ecclesial sphere and the temporal; the order of grace and the order of nature. Both must be upheld. Such an interpretation fits with the imagery of Moses' arms growing heavy, that when he *"lifted up his hands, Israel prevailed. But when he released them a little while, Amalek overcame"* (Ex 17:11). So the battle waxed and waned as the Sign of the Cross was held aloft or not, just as through history the strength of Christendom has depended upon her leaders.

The work of Aaron sharing the Cross calls for all priests to conform themselves to Christ crucified, saying their Mass and Office with attention and devotion daily. And the work of Hur calls for all politicians to conform themselves to Christ crucified, serving justice and truth at whatever cost. If either order slacks, the battle risks being lost. If the state allows transgender hormones for children, what chance have the citizens to defend themselves? If the Church hierarchy allows same-sex blessings in their churches, who can pray there? Thanks be to God, despite low ebbs, the battle will be won.

The Cross is our battle standard! The notion of a standard, or the colours of a regiment, is to keep order during manoeuvres and to provide a rallying point when facing overwhelming force. Christians seeking to be close to the Cross will form a cohesive unit which can stand on the battlefield. A soldier cut off, alone, will flail and fail and die. But men in an orderly formation protect each other's flanks and backs. They defend each other from blows. Each one keeps the enemy forces busy. A Catholic politician who speaks out alone against abortion may well go down. But in a group, in an alliance, with mutual defence and coordination, these can survive to succeed. A priest who does not embrace the Cross in a mortified life, or who imagines Holy Mass to be a festive meal more than a sacrifice, is weak and vulnerable to the blades of the enemy. Embracing the Cross makes one invincible because even in death is victory.

In summary, if our leaders are willing to be crucified for Christ, offering prayers and sacrifices for the whole Church, then Christians will put the enemy to flight.

What of the *"stone"* (Ex 17:12) which was placed under Moses to support him? It is the same word (אֶבֶן) for an altar made of *"stone"*, but uncut (Ex 20:25), which means not the work of human hands. This alludes to Christ, the uncut stone powerful enough to shatter kingdoms into pieces (Dan 2:34). It is also the same word as for the foundation stone upon which Jacob rested his head during his heavenly dream (Gen 28:11), and the stone pillar he anointed with oil (Gen 35:14).[58] In these three usages we

---

[58] The word אֶבֶן is also used for God as *"the stone of Israel"* (Gen 49:24); and for stone tablets upon which the Law was inscribed by God (Ex 24:12).

have Christ, the foot of the Cross and the altar, which three are all in their way the beginning of the Church: Christ absolutely so; the foot of the Cross as the place she began; and the altar as the font of her growth. Putting these together, Moses with arms outstretched on the stone represents Christ's Sacrifice on Calvary being made present at the altar. Therefore the victory already won by Christ on the Cross remains with us to the end of time, especially thanks to our altars.

Hence Moses, after winning the battle, built an altar and said: *"The hand of the throne of the Lord, and the war of the Lord, will be against Amalek from generation to generation"* (Ex 17:16). This is a spiritual war of good against evil that will last to the end of time. That altar was built as a memorial to the victory of God's People, lest we forget the malicious attacks of evil. Now we do not need to travel to Rephidim to encounter this altar. It stands for Holy Mass: *"You, O Lord, endure for eternity, and your memorial is from generation to generation"* (Ps 101:13).

The Cross is the *"Throne of the Lord"* on earth, for on the Cross He wore His thorny crown and above was affixed the title declaring Him King (Mt 27:19; Jn 19:19). Now the same Jesus thrones in Heaven (Heb 1:8; 8:1; Apoc 4:2; 7:17; 12:5). During each Holy Mass the altar brings us into His presence and into the presence of His Sacrifice. This is true not only from *"generation to generation"* in the biological sense, but more significantly in that ascent from our carnal generation to our spiritual generation in Christ. This requires us to fight in the cosmic battle, that is against the evil in ourselves, our own sin. If we do not, then we cannot receive Holy Communion worthily. We do not enter into His Presence.

Such is the meaning of Amalek, his trying to prevent the Israelites from entering the Promised Land. Of his attacks God commanded *"remember"* and *"do not forget"*:

> *Remember what Amalek did to you, along the way, when you were departing from Egypt: how he met you and cut down the stragglers of the troops, who were sitting down, exhausted, when you were consumed by hunger and hardship, and how he did not fear God. Therefore... you shall delete his name from under heaven. Take care not to forget this.* (Dt 26:17-19)

We remember all this in the Mass, consciously or not, for by attending reverently, we pass on the memorial for future generations. We blot out evil by assisting at Holy Mass. We take care not to forget, that for the memorial of the victory, Moses declared: *"The hand of the throne of the Lord..."* so that we may think of Jesus' outstretched arms on the Cross. We have seen how the outstretched arms of Moses on the hill echoes the Crucifixion, and soon will see similar in Samson's arms straining between the pillars. We may be reminded of the Cross whenever the Scriptures speak of the *"mighty, outstretched arm of the Lord"*, also when we see the *Orans* gesture from the priest for the most vital prayers of Holy Mass. These most powerful of prayers include the Oratio, Secret and Post Communion, the Preface, *Te igitur* and much of the Canon and the *Pater noster*, all of which are emphatically prayed 'through Jesus Christ'. The gesture is even more pronounced in the Dominican Rite, when after the consecration of the chalice the celebrant holds his arms out fully extended as if he too is being crucified.

All these prayers, like Moses' prayer on the hilltop, acquire their efficacy from Jesus' Self-Sacrifice on Calvary. Moses was tired on his hilltop; Jesus died on His. Both great leaders saw it through to their people's victory.

We cannot yet see the final victory of Christ over His enemies, of good over evil. But we can remember Moses at Rephidim to know the victory is sure. For each one of us, to share in this victory means to reach Heaven. If we want to know better the way there, we can look even to Moses, for there is, I think, no one else in the OT who by his whole life points so unambiguously to Jesus Christ.

At the end of his *Life of Moses*, St Gregory of Nyssa provokes us to ponder that while it is good and reasonable to wish to avoid the sufferings of hell, it is better to desire the rewards of Heaven. Yet it is better still not to care about going to hell so long as one may serve the salvation of others.[59] Higher still, to desire union with God, friendship with Him, without caring about the rewards of Heaven — for friendship with God, as seen in Moses, is the reward. It inevitably entails helping other souls to reach Heaven. Suffering for God, bringing other people to Him, for His glory, this is the highest friendship and reward. Or what else do we want except that God counted us worthy to serve Him?

Moses served God with increasing intensity for all his 120 years. Deuteronomy tells us he never entered the Promised Land, but was granted to see it only from afar. How is it that the meekest man in the world did not set foot in Israel, was not even

---

[59] Like St Paul, who *"I was desiring that I myself might be anathemized from Christ, for the sake of my brothers, who are my kinsmen according to the flesh"* (Rom 9:3). This is an expression of love, but in fact no one can serve anyone else's salvation except by pursuing their own. The two are never in conflict.

buried there, given that Jesus assures that such inherit the land: *"Blessed are the meek, for they shall possess the earth"* (Mt 5:4). We know the answer. Moses is in Heaven. He has inherited the best Promised Land.

Please God, may Moses now from the supreme heights, with Aaron and Hur, intercede for us down below.

SAMSON DESTROYS THE TEMPLE

Rejoicing in their celebration, having now taken food, they instructed that Samson be called, and that he be mocked before them. And having been brought from prison, he was mocked before them. And they caused him to stand between two pillars. And he said to the boy who was guiding his steps, 'Permit me to touch the pillars, which support the entire house, and to lean against them, so that I may rest a little.' Now the house was full of men and women. And all the leaders of the Philistines were there, as well as about three thousand persons, of both sexes, on the roof and in the upper level of the house, who were watching Samson being mocked. Then, calling upon the Lord, he said, 'O Lord God remember me, and restore to me now my former strength, O my God, so that I may avenge myself against my enemies, and so that I may receive one vengeance for the deprivation of my two eyes.' And taking hold of both the pillars, on which the house rested, and holding one with his right hand and the other with his left, he said, 'May my life die with the Philistines.' And when he had shaken the pillars strongly, the house fell upon all the leaders, and the rest of the multitude who were there. And he killed many more in his death than he had killed before in his life.

— Jdg 16:25-30

If Moses shows us the victory of Christians is absolutely assured, Samson shows us that the defeat of Christ's enemies is equally certain. Although logically the one entails the other, still for our weak, distracted minds it is good to have both definitively portrayed. The same two sides of one single reality are prayed after each Holy Mass: *"the light shines in the darkness, and the darkness did not comprehend it"* (Jn 1:5). It is not two actions, to introduce light and to dispel darkness. It is one action. Also an infusion of sanctifying grace into the soul by Baptism or Confession always entails the obliteration of sin. There is one single act, but both aspects are worth spelling out for our understanding. So having seen Moses and Joshua gain the victory, we see now with Samson not the glory of victory, but the dramatic destruction of the wicked.

Samson prefigures Jesus in his birth, life and death. His miraculous conception and birth were announced to his mother by the message of an angel (Jdg 13:3). Samson was a Nazarene, moved by the Spirit of the Lord (Jdg 13:5; 14:9; 15:14). And as Solomon was the wisest of men until Jesus, so Samson was the strongest until Jesus, gaining easy victories over his enemies for the salvation of his people (Jdg 16:24; 13:5). In the closing chapter of his life, his enemies are seeking to kill him, as they sought to kill Jesus. But it was not so easy to kill him before he was ready to lay down his life. Several times Samson's enemies sought to defeat him in his sleep (Jdg 16:2-21), but Samson overcame sleep as Jesus' overcame death. The first time:

> *Samson slept until the middle of the night, and rising up from there, he took both doors from the gate, with their posts and bars. And laying them upon his shoulders, he carried them to the top of the hill that looks toward Hebron.* (Jdg 16:3)

Shall we think of Jesus carrying His Cross up Calvary when we read Samson, Judge of Israel, carried on his shoulders gateposts and bars, all made of wood, up a hill (Jdg 16:3)? The gate *"posts"* he carries are denoted by the same word (מְזוּזָה / σταθμόν) as the doorposts marked by the blood of the Lamb before the Exodus (Ex 12:7), and their *"bars"* use the same term (בְּרִיחַ / μοχλός) as those which surrounded the tabernacle where God dwells among man (Ex 26:26). Together the posts and bars form the vertical and horizontal of a cross, God among us securing our exodus.

This scene with Samson imaging the Cross and Calvary is bound up with the Resurrection.[60] While Samson was sleeping, his enemies had posted guards all around him *"keeping watch all night"* (Jdg 16:2), just as Jesus' Body was guarded while lying in the tomb. Then for Samson's *"rising up"* (קוּם) in the *"middle of the night"* we have that same root word which in Aramaic Jesus uses for resurrection from the dead (*"Talitha, koumi"* Mk 5:41). Pope St Gregory the Great explains:

> What does the city of Gaza signify, if not hell, the abode of the dead? What is shown by the Philistines, if not the mistaken confidence of the Jews? For, when the Jews saw that the Lord was dead, and His Body placed in the tomb, they posted guards around it. They were delighted that Jesus, Whom the author of life had glorified, was now held captive by the gates of death, just as the Philistines were exultant that they had imprisoned Samson in Gaza.
>
> However, in the middle of the night, Samson not only escaped, but carried the gates away with him. Just so did our Redeemer, rising again before it was light, not only

---

[60] The magnificent twelfth-century Verdun Altar in Stift Klosterneuburg, Austria, depicts Samson carrying the gates of Gaza as corresponding to the Resurrection of Christ.

94

walk free out of death and of hell, but also destroy hell's very gates.[61]

St Cæsarius of Arles observes Samson did not return the gates, signifying death lost its power, and that Jesus going up the hill indicates not Calvary but the Mount of Olives for His Ascension.[62] So the mysteries of Christ's Passion, Resurrection and Ascension are inseparable.

Four times while Samson slept his consort Delilah sought to betray him into the hands of his enemies so that they could kill him. On the third attempt we read of her "fixing with a pin" (וַתִּתְקַע בַּיָּתֵד Jdg 16:14) Samson's woven hair, believing this would rob him of his strength. It sounds innocuous, but these are the same two words used for Jael "driving the peg" into Sisera's skull (וַתִּתְקַע אֶת־הַיָּתֵד Jdg 4:21). The difference is that Samson prefigures Jesus, while Sisera prefigures the Antichrist.[63] That time Samson escaped, Sisera did not. So Jesus overcomes death; the Antichrist will not.

Sick of being betrayed by his lover, Samson chose to surrender himself into the hands of his enemies. He told Delilah the secret of his strength, knowing she would betray him, foreshadowing Jesus knowing He would be betrayed by one who kissed Him, Judas. Here we approach Samson's clearest prefiguration of the Passion of Christ. Not yet forty years old, like Jesus, handed over by a 'friend', tortured and mocked (Jdg 16:5-6; 25-27), we read:

---

[61] Pope St Gregory the Great, *Homily* XXI, 7.

[62] St Cæsarius of Arles, *Sermons,* CXVIII, 5 drawing on St Augustine.

[63] See Fr James Mawdsley, *Crushing satan's head: The Virgin Mary's Victory over the Antichrist Foretold in the Old Testament* (2022).

And taking hold of both the pillars, on which the house rested, and holding one with his right hand and the other with his left, he said, 'May my life die with the Philistines.' And when he had shaken the pillars strongly, the house fell upon all the leaders, and the rest of the multitude who were there. And he killed many more in his death than he had killed before in his life. (Jdg 16:29-30)

Thus the warrior dies, arms fully outstretched left and right, as Moses unmoved by his enemies, as Jesus surrounded by mockers. The Philistines had *"plucked out his eyes"* (Jdg 16:21), which we may take for the connection with sleep-death, being unseeing. The Septuagint uses exactly the same word for Samson leaning on the pillars as for the Lord leaning on Jacob's ladder, which we have already seen depicts the Cross (Jdg 16:29; Gen 28:13). Again the same root is used for the Philistine temple leaning on its pillars (they *"support"* it Jdg 16:26), the house Samson brought down, for Samson leant on them with greater force. For their feast the Philistines' sport cost them their temple and their lives; so for the Pascha the decision of the Sanhedrin would cost them their Temple and their souls.

The final work of this strongest of men was such that *"he killed many more in his death than he had killed before in his life"* (Jdg 16:30). *Mutatis mutandis*, the consummating work of the strongest of all men, our Redeemer Jesus, is that He saved many more by His death than He had healed in His life. So Samson won *"a little rest"* (Jdg 16:26), Jesus won Eternal rest.

Some say Samson the Nazarite is hardly a foreshadowing of Jesus of Nazareth, because his life involved so much violence and sin. But I think he extends hope to all of us, especially those with a messy life, and those who only at the end turn to Christ. St Paul writes that if we die to the world in that we *"consider the things that are above, not the things that are upon the earth... [then] your life is hidden with Christ in God"* (Col 3:2-3). The Scriptures assure us Samson is in Heaven (Heb 11:32). We have seen Christ's life was hidden in Samson. Therefore Samson's life is now *"hidden with Christ in God"*, so we may interpolate, *"When Christ, [our] life, appears, then [Samson] also will appear with Him in glory"* (Col 3:4). The wicked, that is the unrepentant, evidently will not.

Thanks be to God, we are given every chance to repent, as we see next in the Book of Jonah. The short book shows more clearly than Samson that the warfare of life is spiritual, it is against sin, death and hell. It further illustrates that there is no escape from the Cross; yet we should never wish to escape it anyway; rather we ought to always maintain unshakeable hope, even in the most awful of situations, for everything is under God's Providence — sailors, storms, sea beasts and cities — everything is in God's good Hands.

Jonah Sleeps in the Storm

A great tempest took place in the sea, and the ship was in danger of being crushed. And the mariners were afraid, and the men cried out to their god. And they threw the containers that were in the ship into the sea in order to lighten it of them. And Jonah went down into the interior of the ship, and he fell into a painful deep sleep. And the helmsman approached him, and he said to him, 'Why are you weighed down with sleep? Rise, call upon your God, so perhaps God will be mindful of us and we might not perish.' And a man said to his shipmate, 'Come, and let us cast lots, so that we may know why this disaster is upon us.' And they cast lots, and the lot fell upon Jonah. And they said to him: 'Explain to us what is the reason that this disaster is upon us. What is your work? Which is your country? And where are you going? Or which people are you from?' And he said to them, 'I am Hebrew, and I fear the Lord God of heaven, who made the sea and the dry land.' And the men were greatly afraid, and they said to him, 'Why have you done this?' (For the men knew that he was fleeing from the face of the Lord, because he had told them.) And they said to him, 'What are we to do with you, so that the sea will cease for us?' For the sea flowed and swelled. And he said to them, 'Take me, and cast me into the sea, and the sea will cease for you. For I know that it is because of me that this great tempest has come upon you.' And the men were rowing, so as to return to dry land, but they did not succeed. For the sea flowed and swelled against them. And they cried out to the Lord, and they said, 'We beseech you, Lord, do not let us perish for this man's life, and do not attribute to us innocent blood. For you, Lord, have done just as it pleased you.' And they took Jonah and cast him into the sea. And the sea was stilled from its fury. And the men feared the Lord greatly, and they sacrificed victims to the Lord, and they made vows. And the Lord prepared a great fish to swallow Jonah. And Jonah was in the belly of the fish for three days and three nights. And Jonah prayed to the Lord, his God, from the belly of the fish. And he said: 'I cried out to the Lord from my tribulation, and he heeded me. From the belly of hell, I cried out, and you heeded my voice...'

— Jon 1:4-2:3

When a fearsome storm batters a boat at sea, who would fall asleep while everyone else is terrified? Two men: Jesus and Jonah. Jesus calmed the storm with a word (Mk 4:38-40). Jonah calmed the storm by being thrown into it, voluntarily:

Take me, and cast me into the sea, and the sea will cease for you... And they took Jonah and cast him into the sea. And the sea was stilled from its fury. (Jon 1:12-15)

Both episodes point to the fact that Jesus, by freely entering into His Passion, overcomes the storm of death threatening everyone. We can be sure of this interpretation because Our Saviour Himself said:

just as Jonah was in the belly of the whale for three days and three nights, so shall the Son of man be in the heart of the earth for three days and three nights. (Mt 12:40)

Therefore Jonah's sleep in the belly of the boat before descending in the belly of a fish to the belly of the sea mystically figures Christ's sleep on the Cross before descending for three days into the dark depths of death. Only in the light of Christ can we understand the significance of Jonah's *"painful deep sleep"*. It is Jonah's participation in the Passion. Like Christ on Good Friday, Jonah sleeps on wood and in darkness (in the bowels of the ship), though it is day (Mt 27:45).

The word *"painful"* is an unusual translation. The Masoretic text tells us Jonah *"laid down"* (שָׁכַב) and *"fell into a heavy sleep"* (רָדַם). For the first we recall Jesus *"laid down His life for us"* (1 Jn 3:16; cf. Jn 10:11,17-18; 15:13). The second term is not an ordinary *"sleep"*, but is used for Daniel's prophetic sleeps (Dan 8:18; 10:9), as also for those who are floored by divine action: *"At thy rebuke, O God of Jacob, both rider and horse lay stunned"* (Ps 76:6 RSVCE; Vg Ps 75:7). We can imagine Jonah being knocked out by God into a prophetic sleep. The Vulgate tells us Jonah *"was sleeping in a heavy lethargy"* (*dormiebat sopore gravi*). We recall *sopor* is used for Adam and Abraham in their respective prefigurations of the Crucifixion (Gen 2:21; 15:12). In Greek we read that Jonah *"slept and snored"* (ἐκάθευδεν καὶ ἔρρεγχεν) — which some say is how the boat's captain found him. Jonah's was a sleep that called out to the world, like Jesus on the Cross (Mt 27:46).

Emphasised in the account of Jonah's self-sacrifice is the fact that nobody else could save the men on the boat, underscoring that Jesus is our unique Redeemer. All other souls on the ship, afraid of perishing, *"cried out to their god. And they threw the containers that were in the ship into the sea in order to lighten it of them"* (Jon 1:5), but neither their religious fervour nor radical practical efforts were of avail. They had to appeal to the man of God: *"Rise, call upon your God, so perhaps God will be mindful of us and we might not perish"* (Jon 1:6). The shipmaster called upon Jonah as the disciples would call upon Jesus, using the same word for *"perish"* (ἀπόλλυμι, *perire* Lk 8:24), Who immediately answered their prayer, making *"the wind and the raging water"* tranquil. In each Holy Mass when the server pleads *"libera nos a malo"* ("deliver us from evil"), immediately the priest calls upon the Lord to *"Libera nos... ab omnibus malis"* (*"deliver us, we beseech Thee, O Lord, from all evils"*).[64] The Lord hears all these prayers and is not slow to act, though we might not see it.

Our participation in Calvary through the Mass, our Faith, is to be rational, with understanding (*Quam oblationem;* Rom 12:1). So the mariners put to Jonah the profound and urgent questions which confront all in tribulation: *"Explain to us what is the reason that this disaster is upon us?"* — why is there evil and death in the world? *"What is your work?"* — what is the operation, the mission of the Christ, the chosen one of God, for *"they cast lots, and the lot fell upon Jonah"* (Jon 1:7)? *"Which is your country?"* — what is the origin of the Messiah, the Son of God? *"Where are you going?"* — what is His final purpose? *"Which people are you from?"* — which souls are with Him? Jonah answers all their questions, the summary of which is given to us in one packed sentence: *"I am Hebrew, and I fear the Lord God of heaven, who made the sea and the dry land"* (Jon 1:9). This calls for understanding!

Jonah identifies himself as *"Hebrew"* (עִבְרִי). Here he traces his roots back almost two thousand years. The Hebrews were the

---

[64] Earlier in the Mass the priest had prayed *"preserve us from eternal damnation"* (*Hanc igitur*).

people Moses led in the Exodus, called out of Egypt by God. Their Passover feast distinguished them from all *"foreigners"* who were not allowed to eat it (Ex 12:43). The sense of exclusion was mutual. Hundreds of years earlier, when Joseph's brothers visited him, even as honoured guests they had to feast separately from the locals, *"for it is unlawful for Egyptians to eat with Hebrews, and they consider feasting in this way to be profane"* (Gen 43:32). Before this, in prison Joseph knew his identity was important, explaining he was *"stolen from the land of the Hebrews"* (Gen 40:15; cf. 41:12). Before this, Potiphar's wife saw it as a term of contempt: *"the Hebrew slave"* (Gen 39:14,17), as a 'foreigner'. Her insult was the second time in history the word is recorded.

The very first time is in describing *"Abraham the Hebrew"* (Gen 14:13). At that time he lived in Hebron, but the word *"Hebrew"* indicates 'sojourner'. Abraham and his family dwelt in tents, or tabernacles (Gen 13:18; 33:17; Heb 11:9). In this place the Septuagint, rather than call Abraham *"the Hebrew"*, calls him *"the traveller"* (dative: περάτη). It is significant for the man of faith who believes we sojourn on this earth before passing over to a better one.

The root word is likely Heber (עֵבֶר), the great-great-great-great-grandfather of Abraham (Gen 10:25). The Torah specifically notes that Heber is descended from Shem, the son first blessed by Noah, calling him *"Shem, the father of all the sons of Heber"* (Gen 10:21). These are the Semites whose explorations went east beyond the River Euphrates. Hence some think the name 'Heber' means one who 'passed over' the great river. Again, very fitting for the People of the Exodus (cf. Passover), passing over the great river (cf. Jordan) or death. Jonah was well aware that he was no Ninevite, no Goy, no ordinary man.

The only Person who Self-consciously identifies His roots as going further back than Heber, or Shem, is Jesus. Scores of times He called Himself the 'Son of Man', thinking of Adam, whose name means 'man' (אָדָם). He also was a sojourner: *"Foxes have dens, and the birds of the air have nests, but the Son of man has nowhere to rest His head"* (Mt 8:20), Who 'passed over' death. He was no ordinary man, but *"was of Adam, who was of God"* (Lk 3:38).

This is the God Jonah wisely feared, saying: *"I am Hebrew, and I fear the Lord God of heaven, who made the sea and the dry land"* (Jon 1:9). He refers to One even more ancient than Heber, One active from the beginning: the *"Lord"* (mentioned eleven times in Gen 2), *"God"* (fourteen times in Gen 2; thirty-three times in Gen 1), of *"heaven"* (ten times in Gen 1), who *"made"* (seven times in Gen 1) the *"sea"* (four times in Gen 1) and *"dry land"* (twice in Gen 1). All this pointedly distinguishes the True God, the Creator, from false gods, from creatures who cannot save (Acts 14:14).

How important to Jonah is that term *"the dry land"* (יַבָּשָׁה, ξηρά, *arida* — Gen 1:9; Jon 1:9)![65] It is the 'dry land' upon which the Hebrews walked out of captivity when God divided the Red Sea (Ex 14:16), and the 'dry land' upon which the Hebrews walked into the Promised Land when God halted the Jordan River (Josh 4:22-23). The 'dry land' signifies life, contrasted with the sea, the waters of death. He Who can make the dry land is Lord of life and death. He is to be feared. As the sailors received great

---

[65] *"Dry land"* as distinct from *"earth"* *"land"* (אֶרֶץ , γῆν, *terra* Gen 1:1).

answers from Jonah, so we ought to hear the great answers of Jesus Christ, until we see that He is our Saviour, God from God, sent to redeem us from sin and from sinking traceless into dissolution as a ship in a storm.

But we are slow to understand, as were the sailors. Disconcerted by Jonah's apparently inhumane instructions to throw him overboard, they seek to overcome death by their own efforts: *"the men were rowing, so as to return to dry land, but they did not succeed. For the sea flowed and swelled against them"* (Jon 1:13). They want to *"return to dry land"*, to our condition before the Fall. Likewise today we have men obsessed with finding a biological intervention to achieve immortality. But there is no other way; Jesus is the sole Mediator. His Way we must accept:

> *We beseech you, Lord, do not let us perish for this man's life, and do not attribute to us innocent blood. For you, Lord, have done just as it pleased you.* (Jon 1:14; Mt 27:25)

So they *"took Jonah and cast him into the sea. And the sea was stilled from its fury"* (Jon 1:15). St Jerome teaches this is a figure of Christ's Passion.[66] The Sacrifice of Christ is propitiatory, beloved of God, appeasing His wrath, saving us. It provokes us to reverence and unites us with God: *"the men feared the Lord greatly, and they sacrificed victims to the Lord, and they made vows"* (Jon 1:16).

Meanwhile *"Jonah prayed to the Lord, his God, from the belly of the fish"* (Jon 2:2). So Jesus' communication with the Godhead was not severed by death. Through the Hypostatic Union His

---

[66] St Jerome, *Commentary on St Matthew's Gospel*, I.

Body, Blood and Soul all remained in contact with His Divinity (albeit not with each other). Jonah begins his prayer by twice saying he knows he is heard. It is a prayer of confidence. So Jesus going into death never doubted He would overcome it:

> *I cried out to the Lord from my tribulation, and he heeded me. From the belly of hell, I cried out, and you heeded my voice... And I said: I am expelled from the sight of your eyes. Yet, truly, I will see your holy temple again. The waters surrounded me, even to the soul. The abyss has walled me in. The ocean has covered my head... The bars of the earth have enclosed me forever. And you will raise up my life from corruption, Lord, my God.* (Jon 2:3-7)

Jonah went where God 'dwelt not' (*"I am expelled from the sight of your eyes"*), yet stated he would see the Temple again. In this he gives a clear expression of the Resurrection, according to the same interpretation which SS Peter and Paul give the Psalm which the prophet Jonah echoed: *"For you will not abandon my soul to hell, nor will you allow your holy one to see corruption"* (Ps 15:10; Acts 2:31; 13:35). Hearing his prayer, *"the Lord spoke to the fish, and it vomited Jonah onto dry land"* (Jn 2:11). Translation: *"And the Lord spoke"* — which is how He operates — *"to the fish"* — God commands the works of death and they obey Him — *"and it vomited Jonah"* — death cannot assimilate being, for non-being is pure privation, not a dualistic principle in opposition to Being — *"onto dry land"* — land not flooded, the land of the living, that place where the waters of death do not reach. Three days after prefiguring the Passion in his sleep, Jonah prefigured the Resurrection by his return to dry land.

"And the word of the Lord came to Jonah a second time, saying: Rise, and go to Nineveh, the great city" (Jon 3:1-2). Again Jonah is told: *"Rise"* (קוּם / ἀνάστηθι), resurrect! His life is rich in prefiguring Christ.

God commanded him: *"preach in [Nineveh] the preaching that I say to you"* (Jon 3:2). Jonah obeyed, and as a sign that Jesus' preaching would reach the world we read: *"And the men of Nineveh believed in God... "* (Jon 3:5). *Credo in unum Deum...*

The world believes, and the world repents. From Nineveh's king down to its cattle, they desisted from food and water and were *"covered with sackcloth"* (Jn 3:8). They cried out to the Lord, repenting their sins, resolving to do penance in order not to *"perish"* (Jon 3:9). God saw their works, their conversion, and had mercy. They did not *"perish"*.

It was precisely for this reason, not to *"perish"* (אָבַד, ἀπόλλυμι, *perire*), that the captain of the ship came to Jonah, and for which the sailors had all prayed, and now the entirety of Nineveh (Jon 1:6,14; 3:9). We see Jonah's passion saved others from sinking into death, and through this his continuation afterwards of his mission achieves its purpose of saving many more. In Jesus' case, while on the Cross He saved a thief and a soldier, and afterwards thanks to the Cross, working through His Apostles and their successors, Jesus saved many, many more.

So rich is Sacred Scripture, we find Jonah prefiguring the Crucifixion once again outside the great city, Nineveh, as Christ was crucified outside the city, Jerusalem (cf. Heb 13:12). Inadvertently pre-echoing Christ, Jonah declared to God: *"now, Lord, I ask you to take my life from me. For it is better for me to die than to live"* (Jon 4:3). The willingness to die is the link with Jesus, albeit in Jonah from frustration. Instead God caused a kind of tree to grow, and Jonah sat in its shadow (as Elijah in the shade of the juniper tree, as Jerusalem went dark on Good Friday). Presumably that night Jonah slept. In any case, it was the tree that died, not he. A kind of death of the Cross. And all this to teach him — to teach us — the care God has for ignorant men, His desire to save us:

> shall I not spare Nineveh, the great city, in which there are more than one hundred and twenty thousand men, who do not know the difference between their right and their left, and many beasts? (Jon 4:11).

Sounds like the world today. In this context, it is significant that Jonah repeated: "It is better for me to die than to live" (Jon 4:8). On Christ's lips these words are pure love (cf. Jn 16:7).

On its own, Jonah's life is exceedingly strange. In Christ his life is awesome. Is he presented as a problematic character in the Bible? Then he is certainly a deeply humble man, for no one else could have passed on his story to us except himself. No one else could have known the various parts. He told his story in a way which gives no glory to himself. Rather he reserved all glory for Him in Whom he had faith.

Hearing Jesus now, with our hearts open, let us not be blind to the *"sign of Jonah"* (Mt 12:39-41), nor deaf to the preaching of One *"greater than Jonah"* (Lk 11:29-32).[67] Jesus, the Lord, is Risen. He calls us to repent (Mt 4:17; Lk 5:32).

------

[67] St Ambrose, *Homilies on St Luke's Gospel*, VII, 8, 97 "Furthermore, the sign of Jonas, while it typifies our Lord's Passion, also testifies to the gravity of the sins the Jews committed. Notice here too both a declaration of authority and a token of mercy. For in the example of the Ninevites Christ both threatens the penalty and indicates the remedy. And so even the Jews have no reason to despair of forgiveness if they are willing to do penance."

As I live, says the Lord God, I do not desire the death of the impious, but that the impious should convert from his way and live. (Ezek 33:11)

Our repentance involves embracing the Cross. It is a weapon directed at overcoming the snare of sin, the grip of death and the hold of hell.

This war is interior, hidden, before it is exterior, bloody. Jonah's experience reassures those who taste the Cross to trust God in all circumstances, no matter how horrifying they seem. In any case the Cross cannot be escaped. Jonah tried, but God found him, judging it better for all that his mission be completed. If we find we cannot avoid the Cross, even visiting the belly of hell, we can trust God is using it for the good of many.

SAUL SAVED IN SLEEP

And David said: 'As the Lord lives, unless the Lord himself will strike him... I may not extend my hand against the Christ of the Lord. Now therefore, take the spear that is at his head, and the jug of water, and let us go.' And so, David took the spear, and the jug of water that was at Saul's head, and they went away. And there was no one who saw it, or knew it, or awakened, but they were all sleeping. For a deep sleep from the Lord had fallen over them. And when David had crossed over to the opposite side, and had stood upon the top of the hill far away, so that there was a great interval between them, David cried out to the people, and to Abner, the son of Ner, saying, 'Will you not respond, Abner?' And responding, Abner said, 'Who are you, that you would cry out and disquiet the king?' And David said to Abner: 'Are you not a man? And who else is like you in Israel? Then why have you not guarded your lord the king? For one of the people entered, so that he might kill the king, your lord. This is not good, what you have done. As the Lord lives, you are sons of death, because you have not guarded your lord, the Christ of the Lord. Now therefore, where is the king's spear, and where is the jug of water that was at his head?' Then Saul recognised the voice of David, and he said, 'Is this not your voice, my son David?' And David said, 'It is my voice, my lord the king... For what reason does my lord persecute his servant? What have I done? Or what evil is there in my hand? Now therefore, listen, I beg you, my lord the king, to the words of your servant. If the Lord has stirred you up against me, let the sacrifice be fragrant. But if the sons of men have done so, they are accursed in the sight of the Lord, who has cast me out this day, so that I would not live within the inheritance of the Lord, saying, "Go, serve strange gods." And now, let not my blood be poured out upon the earth before the Lord. For the king of Israel has gone out, so that he might seek a flea, just as the partridge is pursued amid the mountains.' And Saul said: 'I have sinned. Return, my son David. For I will never again do evil to you, because my life has been precious in your eyes this day. For it is apparent that I have acted senselessly, and have been ignorant of very many things.' And responding, David said: 'Behold, the king's spear. Let one of the servants of the king cross over and take it. And the Lord will repay each one according to his justice and faith. For the Lord has delivered you this day into my hand, but I was not willing to extend my hand against the Christ of the Lord. And just as your soul has been magnified this day in my eyes, so let my soul be magnified in the eyes of the Lord, and may he free me from all distress.' Then Saul said to David: 'You are blessed, my son David. And whatever you may do, it shall certainly succeed.' And David departed on his way. And Saul returned to his place.

— 1 Sam 26:11-25

The Cross is a living battle standard. If we gaze upon it, ponder it in the Scriptures and in life, it teaches us how to fight. The method involves mercy. The more merciful one is to one's enemy, the more fruit the Cross will yield.

By this means David went from being *"a flea... a partridge... pursued amid the mountains"* (1 Sam 26:20) to being crowned King of Israel. Saul already understood all this from a previous incident where David gratuitously spared his life.[68] That Saul also survives his sleep thanks to David's reverence, when David might have repaid the unjust attacks Saul launched against him, conveys that the Cross is aimed at reconciliation: *"For certainly God was in Christ, reconciling the world to Himself, not charging them with their sins"* (2 Cor 5:19). Alas Saul, although he saw the truth of the Cross, repenting his evil and speaking words of reconciliation, soon put it out of his mind (1 Sam 26:21). He rejected the way of the Cross. He died defeated.

The rare phrase for the deep sleep which the Lord let fall upon Adam and Abram is also used regarding Saul, for *"a deep sleep from the Lord had fallen over them"* (1 Sam 26:12). Is it coincidence that the same verse mentions a spear and water? And is it coincidence that here David accuses the mighty of Israel: *"As the Lord lives, you are sons of death, because you have not guarded your lord, the Christ of the Lord"* (1 Sam 26:16), and specifically draws everyone's attention to the spear and the water?

---

[68] Saul *"said to David: 'You are more just than I am. For you have distributed good to me, but I have repaid evil to you. And you have revealed this day the good that you have done for me: how the Lord delivered me into your hand, but you did not kill me. For who, when he will have found his enemy, will release him along a good path? So may the Lord repay you for this good turn, because you have acted on my behalf this day. And now I know certainly that you shall be king, and you shall have the kingdom of Israel in your hand. Swear to me in the Lord that you will not take away my offspring after me, nor take away my name from the house of my father.' And David swore to Saul. Therefore, Saul went away to his own house. And David and his men ascended to places that were more secure"* (1 Sam 24:18-22).

The last sentence here is especially instructive: by mercy we rise toward God.

Soon after this we read of blood *"poured out upon the earth before the Lord. For the king of Israel"* (1 Sam 26:20), and again David tells us, *"Behold, the king's spear"* (1 Sam 26:22). Surely this repeated mention of the Lord, His Christ, the king, the spear and water and blood, all of it introduced with that signature phrase of *"a deep sleep from the Lord"*, is cumulatively to recall to us the Crucifixion.

If so, then this attempt by David to reconcile with Saul is more profoundly about the New and the Old Covenant, showing, as does all David's behaviour toward Saul (cf. 1 Sam 24), that Christians ought never to seek vengeance or harm against the Jews. Rather as Pope Callixtus II commanded in his twelfth-century Bull *Sicut Judæis*, when the Church was ascending to the height of political influence, Christians should grant protection to the Jews, who should suffer no prejudice, no violence against person or property, no extortion by the hands of Christians, no damage to their graveyards, no pressure to be baptised. Numerous popes before and after him decreed similarly.

It is worth reviewing in this light the magnificent dialogue between David and Saul:

> *Then David had crossed over to the opposite side, and had stood upon the top of the hill far away, so that there was a great interval between them, David cried out to the people...* (1 Sam 26:13ff)

Is this Jesus Who took the spear in His Heart, Who *"crossed over to the opposite side"* of death, Who *"upon the top of the hill far away"* — Calvary — *"so that there was a great interval between them... cried out to the people..."*? Is there not a great gulf between Christians and Jews today? Does not David cry out to the people who are encamped against him? Are Christians really excluded from the inheritance of Israel, falsely accused of serving *"strange gods"* (1 Sam 26:19)? Yet with David they indeed honour the throne which endures forever.

At last relenting, *"Saul recognised the voice of David, and he said, 'Is this not your voice, my son David?'"* (1 Sam 26:17). Responding David now asks: *"For what reason does my lord persecute his servant? What have I done? Or what evil is there in my hand?"* (1 Sam 26:18). The fulness of this question is Jesus asking from Heaven: *"Saul, Saul, why are you persecuting Me?"* (Acts 9:4) David's submission is fulfilled in Christ: in so far as the Lord allowed persecution, the sacrifice was indeed *"fragrant"*; in so far as it came from the hearts of men, *"they are accursed"* (1 Sam 26:19). Jesus did not harm His persecutors, and the Lord was pleased to free Him from death, or in David's case, *"from all distress"* (1 Sam 26:24). Such perfect love conquers:

> Saul said: '*I have sinned. Return, my son David. For I will never again do evil to you, because my life has been precious in your eyes this day...* ' (1 Sam 26:21)

A final word on the spear: *"David said: 'Behold, the king's spear... And the Lord will repay each one according to his justice and faith"* (1 Sam 26:22-23). In the end Saul was repaid by the spear in a way which spoke of Christ. The Septuagint uses exactly the same word for the Lord *"leaning"* on the ladder of which Jacob dreamt, and for blinded Samson *"leaning"* on the pillars he brought down, which are both prefigurations of the Crucifixion, as it does for wounded Saul *"leaning"* on this spear when *"anguish had seized"* him at the time of his death.[69] Alas, it does not seem he had faith. He was unwilling to risk his life be taken by scoffers as Jesus' life would be, telling his armour bearer:

> *Draw your sword and strike me, otherwise these uncircumcised may come and kill me, mocking me. And his armour bearer was not willing...* (1 Sam 31:4)

High on the mountain, exhausted and wounded, King Saul opted for a self-immolation as tragic for him as the mass suicide at Masada. This though is not the image of the Cross. It is David who reveals the meaning of the Cross.

Calvary is at the centre of the battlefield: those who look upon it and see God's love, who are moved to detest their sin, will live like those who looked on the serpent raised in the desert did live (Num 21:6-9). Those who will not look, who refuse to understand, who choose to forget what they see, they die. Realising the mercy God has had on us, how can we be unmerciful? Jesus stated: *"With whatever measure you have measured out, it shall be measured back to you, and more shall be added to you"* (Mk 4:24). If we dish out evil, it will be repaid with due interest.

More interestingly, what opportunities life provides to dish out mercy! Then attacks upon us become powerful means to develop humility, to grow in faith, to imitate Christ as did David:

> *O Lord, my God, if there is iniquity in my hands, if I have done this: if I have repaid those who rendered evils to me, may I deservedly fall away empty before my enemies: let the enemy pursue my soul, and take hold of it, and trample my*

---

[69] "ἐπεστήρικτο" Gen 28:13; Jdg 26:29; 2 Sam 1:6,10.

life into the earth, and drag down my glory into the dust.
(Ps 7:4-6)

David would rather be on the Cross than crucify his enemy, understanding he too is made in the image of God. Though speaking specifically of Saul, the anointed king of Israel, David's words make us mindful that to crucify anyone entails crucifying Christ: *"I was not willing to extend my hand against the Christ of the Lord"* (1 Sam 26:23; cf. 1 Sam 24:11,12; 26:9,11).

King David knows all about the Cross.

DAVID'S ECSTASY

> *Unto the end. A Psalm for David in an ecstasy... Into your hands, I commend my spirit.*
>
> — Ps 30:1,6 (DRB)

Psalm 30 is entitled in the Septuagint and Vulgate: *"Unto the end, a psalm for David, in an ecstasy"*. The Septuagint uses this word *"ecstasy"* for the deep sleeps of Adam and Abraham, so we may consider the Passion.[70] For a prophet an ecstasy is a withdrawal from the everyday world, a visionary dream or experience, standing outside of oneself (ἔκ-στασις, *ex-stasis*). Amazingly, Dionysius writes that "God Himself suffered ecstasy through love."[71] He explains that God's love for His Creation is so intense that God pours Himself out in order to enter into Creation. This always infinite love took off on the Cross to exceed all description, being revealed as excessive in the moment of death like a singularity on a mathematical curve.

David was chosen to enter into this ecstasy. Here he looked, somehow, upon the Passion of Christ, for in Psalm 30 he quotes Jesus' words from the Cross: *"Into thy hands I commend my spirit"* (Lk 23:46; Ps 30:6 DRB). It is not that Jesus on the Cross thought it opportune to quote His ancestor of one thousand years' blessed memory. Rather the Crucifixion was the centre of God's eternal Plan, and David was given a preview in the Spirit of Jesus' prayer. This is not strictly speaking a prefiguration but a prophetic

---

[70] "καὶ ἐπέβαλεν ὁ θεὸς ἔκστασιν ἐπὶ τὸν Αδαμ" (Gen 2:21).

"ἔκστασις ἐπέπεσεν τῷ Αβραμ" (Gen 15:12).

[71] Dionysius the Areopagite, *The Divine Names*, IV, 13.

vision. With the whole of Psalm 30, David tells us the Crucifixion is not a moment of despair, but of full confidence in God's Salvation:

In you, Lord, I have hoped; let me never be confounded. In your justice, deliver me. Incline your ear to me. Hasten to rescue me. Be for me a protector God and a house of refuge, so as to accomplish my salvation... You will lead me out of this snare, which they have hidden for me... Into your hands, I commend my spirit. You have redeemed me, O Lord, God of truth... I will exult and rejoice in your mercy. For you have looked upon my humility; you have saved my soul from constraint. And you have not enclosed me in the hands of the enemy. You have set my feet in a spacious place. (Ps 30:2-9)

"I will exult and rejoice" is the prayer from the Cross, for *"You will lead me out of this snare"*. Like David, looking to Jesus, we can pray the same in every tribulation, if we have a share in their *"humility"*, which is the reason *"you have saved my soul from constraint. And you have not enclosed me in the hands of the enemy"*. Even if in dire difficulties we actually die, still the Cross is the way to absolute freedom: *"You have set my feet in a spacious place"* — Heaven. This hope in God is all the more meaningful for the depths of suffering from which it arises:

Lord... I am troubled. My eye has been disturbed by wrath, along with my soul and my gut. For my life has fallen into sorrow, and my years into sighing... I have become a disgrace among all my enemies, and even more so to my neighbours, and a dread to my acquaintances. Those who catch sight of me, flee away from me. I have become forgotten, like one dead to the heart. I have become like a damaged utensil. For I have heard the harsh criticism of many who linger in the area. While assembled together against me in that place, they deliberated on how to take away my life. But I have hoped in you, O Lord. I said, 'You are my God.' My lots are in your hands. Rescue me from the hand of my enemies and from those who are persecuting me. (Ps 30:10-16)

Jesus too was abandoned by His friends and surrounded by insulting enemies. *"I have become forgotten, like one dead to the heart"*. How terrible to be forgotten. But the night before He died, Jesus established an everlasting memorial to His Passion, commanding those who loved Him: *"This is My Body, which is given for you. Do this as a commemoration of Me"* (Lk 22:19). So He is never forgotten; nor, after being an outcast, was David. Withdrawing from the world serves intimacy with God, as the Psalm indicates:

Shine your face upon your servant. Save me in your mercy. Do not let me be confounded... How great is the multitude of your sweetness, O Lord, which you keep hidden for those who fear you, which you have perfected for those who hope in you, in the sight of the sons of men. You hide them in the concealment of your face, from the disturbance of men. You protect them in your tabernacle, from the contradiction of tongues. Blessed is the Lord. For he has shown his wonderful mercy to me, in a fortified city. (Ps 30:17-22)

Such are His thoughts on the Cross: *"Save me"*... and *"Blessed is the Lord. For he has shown his wonderful mercy to me, in a fortified city"*. This city is the Church, the New Jerusalem, where we are protected *"in your tabernacle"*. Like the Holy Eucharist, we may perceive damage or corruption or even sacrilege against the external appearances of the Host, but nothing can harm the inner substance. So also a man might suffer every kind of injury, insult and abuse, but maintain his love of God entirely intact. As Son of God Jesus is impassible, cannot suffer. As Son of Man He suffered maximally and trusted entirely. He did this to redeem us, and to give us an example so we, in ecstasy, might imitate Him:

> But I said in the excess [ecstasy] of my mind: 'I have been cast away from the glance of your eyes.' And so, you heeded the voice of my prayer, while I was still crying out to you. Love the Lord, all you his saints. For the Lord will require truth, and he will abundantly repay those who act with arrogance. Act manfully, and let your heart be strengthened, all you who hope in the Lord. (Ps 30:23-25)

This standing firm is not a matter of the body or the emotions, which might be in shreds, nor even a matter of our thoughts, which in *"the excess of my mind"* can entertain errors, frightening us with the suggestion that we *"have been cast away from the glance of your eyes"*, even though the will taking counsel on the idea does not consent to it.[72] For our sanctuary, our invincible citadel, is the will: it is to simply decide to 'cry out' to God no matter what, to *"Love the Lord"* regardless of our fate, then with nothing left to lose will the *"heart be strengthened"*.

---

[72] St Thomas, *S.Th.* II-I, Q.15 a.3.

If we read Psalm 30 rightly then we will not be misled by the opening of Psalm 21 (*"O God, my God, look upon me. Why have you forsaken me?"*) into thinking God had ever *"forsaken"* His Son. One only has to read the whole of Psalm 21, with its triumphant ending, to see this is an impossible error to ascribe to Jesus. Rather He is condescending to our sense of abandonment, to reach us even there. Even if we feel forsaken, even if we think we are abandoned, we are not, so let the heart remain true to God. David's Psalms taken together give all the proof we need.

Other Psalms deal closely with the Passion, the most celebrated being Ps 21; 33; 54; 68; 108. Remaining though by the theme of *'sleeps'* as figures for Christ's Passion, we will search other Psalms.

"Arise, why sleepest thou, O Lord?" (Ps 43:23 DRB) *"I have slept and taken my rest: and I have risen up, because the Lord hath protected me"* (Ps 3:6 DRB). Is this not the Resurrection? It would scarcely be worth remembering for 3,000 years if it were not. Similarly the Psalmist implores God that enemies not prevail *"lest I fall asleep forever in death"* (Ps 12:4). Not that Jesus expected God would prevent His enemies putting Him to death, but that it not be *"forever"*, praying instead He would awake from even this deepest of sleeps. His enemies denied His Resurrection in advance, as did Judas who had heard of it directly from Jesus' own lips, but Jesus knew the Psalms better:

All my enemies were whispering against me. They were thinking up evils against me. They established an unjust word against me. Will he that sleeps no longer rise again (לָקוּם / ἀναστῆναι / resurgat)? For even the man of my peace, in whom I hoped, who ate my bread, has greatly supplanted me. But you, O Lord, have mercy on me, and raise me up again (וַהֲקִימֵנִי / ἀνάστησόν / *resuscita). And I will requite them.* (Ps 40:8-11)

As in this Psalm 'rising again' and being 'resuscitated' have connotations with 'resurrection' in Hebrew, Latin and Greek, then it is fair on reading *"he that sleeps"* to think of death.

If in Noah, Lot and Boaz we recognise inebriation points to Christ's Passion, then reading Psalm 77, wherein the Lord awakes *"like a mighty man after being surfeited with wine"*, in fury routing his foes, we see there is no more apt application than Jesus in His Resurrection, His Victory over His enemies:

And the Lord was awaked as one out of sleep, and like a mighty man that hath been surfeited with wine. And he smote his enemies on the hinder parts: he put them to an everlasting reproach. (Ps 77:65-66 DRB)

The Psalms are, in places, notoriously obscure. This is by God's design — clerics and religious who pray the 150 Psalms every week can never claim to exhaust them. Not even David can have understood everything he sang. But while, unlike Jesus, we can scarcely uncover the Passion by studying the Psalms, we can, already knowing His Passion, look back on the Psalms and in them identify the Passion. The obscurity of suffering, of injustice, of cruelty, may be turned to light in the Lord. Among the strongest themes in the Psalter is: *"This poor man cried, and the Lord heard him: and saved him out of all his troubles"*. But the main theme is: *"Praise God"*. Combining these two the Spirit whispers to us: Trust God, poor man, and praise Him, no matter the tribulations!

"How great is the multitude of your sweetness, O Lord, which you keep hidden for those who fear you" (Ps 30:20). To revisit an example of this multitude: David once sang in Christ, *"Into thy hands I commit my spirit"* (Ps 30). A thousand years later, Jesus said the same on the Cross, then St Stephen did likewise as he gave his life in Christ (Acts 7:59). Now two thousand years later these words are said all around the world every evening at Compline just before the *Nunc dimittis*. They provide, just before we fall asleep, a spiritual practice for our death. If we mean what we pray, then we are prepared to die in the night. It could happen. If we are not prepared for that, then the prayer provokes us to examine our conscience, to forgive everyone who has ever wronged us, and to call on God's mercy. Then we are ready for death. So many souls assisted by David's heartfelt prayer.

This is a gentle note on which to end the chapter on battle. The Cross assures the victory of the good as with Moses; and the defeat of evil as by Samson; and saves many lives from hell as Jonah shows; and its method of mercy is vastly rewarding as demonstrated by David. The Cross is something to be desired every day rather than avoided. Again thanks in part to David, God gives us tools to explore it through prayer, rather than only through pain. When Jesus was mocked: *"If Thou be the Son of God, come down from the Cross"* (Mt 27:40 DRB), He was, of course, not tempted. He knew the triumph of the Cross. For this He was born to us.

THE FRUIT

OF THE TREE

W hether we will end in Heaven or hell depends upon how we respond to the substance of the Holy Eucharist.[73] If we have reverence for this Most Blessed Sacrament then God gives us life. If we ill-treat It, we condemn ourselves to death. Jesus paid a great price to teach this, suffering meekly to soften our hearts. Although these points are made plain in the NT, many Catholics remain blind to them. To help convince those who care to seek, God has planted the seeds of these truths marvellously in the OT.

That our final judgement depends upon our treatment of the Holy Eucharist is delicately woven into the story of Joseph. That Holy Communion is the real bread of life we find with Elijah. That to profane the Sacrament means death is illustrated in Lot's daughters. And a costly warning against becoming hard-hearted in

---

[73] For the unevangelised, their response to Jesus Christ as *Logos*, as expressed by the natural law, is the testing ground.

this regard is given by Ezekiel. Before exploring these four sometimes dark accounts, here is some bright illumination from the NT:

Our estimation of the Holy Eucharist, or more generally the Word of the Cross, leads to Heaven or hell:

> *For the Word of the Cross is certainly foolishness to those who are perishing. But to those who have been saved, that is, to us, it is the power of God.* (1 Cor 1:18)

Holy Communion is nourishment unto eternal life:

> *Jesus said to them: 'Amen, amen, I say to you, unless you eat the Flesh of the Son of man and drink His Blood, you will not have life in you. Whoever eats My Flesh and drinks My Blood has eternal life, and I will raise him up on the last day. For My Flesh is true food, and My Blood is true drink.'* (Jn 6:54-56)

Receiving Holy Communions unworthily is condemned:

> *For whenever you eat this bread and drink this cup, you proclaim the death of the Lord, until He returns. And so, whoever eats this bread, or drinks from the cup of the Lord, unworthily, shall be liable of the Body and Blood of the Lord... Whoever eats and drinks unworthily, eats and drinks a sentence against himself, not discerning it to be the Body of the Lord.* (1 Cor 11:26-29)

No matter the cost, it is necessary to embrace the Cross:

> *Whoever loves father or mother more than Me is not worthy of Me. And whoever loves son or daughter above Me is not*

worthy of Me. Whoever does not take up his Cross and follow Me is not worthy of Me. Whoever finds his life, will lose it. And whoever will have lost his life because of Me, shall find it. (Mt 10:37-39)

For ancient demonstrations of these truths, first we go to Joseph.

JOSEPH JUDGE OF DREAMS

'We have seen a dream, and there is no one to interpret it for us.' And Joseph said to them, 'Doesn't interpretation belong to God? Recount for me what you have seen.' The chief cupbearer explained his dream first... Joseph responded: 'This is the interpretation of the dream. The three shoots are the next three days... Only remember me, when it will be well with you... For I have been stolen from the land of the Hebrews, and here, innocently, I was cast into the pit.' The chief miller of grain, seeing that he had wisely unraveled the dream, said: 'I also saw a dream...'

— Gen 40:8-16

Before investigating how Joseph is a type of Jesus as Judge, it helps to recognise the broader way by which Joseph, the favourite son of Israel, prefigures Jesus, the beloved Son in Whom the Father is *"well pleased"* (Mt 3:17; 17:5).

In outline, it is written of Joseph that *"everyone should bend their knee before him"* (Gen 41:43), who was named the *"saviour of the world"* (Gen 41:45), because he gave bread whose *"bounty exceeded all measure"* (Gen 41:49; 54-55) to *"bring about the salvation of many peoples"* (Gen 50:20; Acts 4:12). All this speaks of Jesus. His very Name means 'Saviour' (Mt 1:21), before Whom *"every knee shall bow"* (Phil 2:10), Who gives daily the super-substantial Bread (Mt 6:11), His own *"Flesh, for the life of the world"* (Jn 6:52), the Holy Eucharist. Prefiguring Jesus, Joseph reached his position as saviour through suffering a long passion ordained by God.[74] This included enduring murderous envy from his brothers, being thrown into a pit (symbolic of death), being falsely accused (Gen 39:14) and imprisoned.

Despite his exceptionally good and fruitful labours, Joseph incurred the baneful enmity of Potiphar's wife. In this she may stand for the Sanhedrin of Jesus' time, because she is wedded to worldly power (Potiphar) and accuses Joseph of the very thing which she had been unsuccessfully trying to tempt him to do — *"Sleep with me"* (Gen 39:7-17).[75] In its turn the Sanhedrin wanted a worldly Messiah to deliver them from Rome, yet they accused Jesus of this very thing which He had demonstrably refused to do (to lead the Jews as a political king against Caesar). Moreover the Sanhedrin accused Jesus of violating the Law of Moses and of threatening to destroy the Temple. But they themselves savaged the Law of Moses (Mt 23), especially in the illegal trial of Jesus, and they tore down the actual Temple, His Body, though of course He resurrected it. Completing the parallel, we may say that if worldly desire of Potiphar's wife corresponds with that of the Sanhedrin in Jesus' time, then Joseph's unimpeachable chastity speaks of Jesus' faithful focus on His divine mission. He would not be seduced from it.

---

[74] Gen 39:23; 45:5-8; 50:19-20.

[75] The word שָׁכַב, generally meaning 'to lie down' or 'sleep', is used 21 times in Genesis: seven times when Lot's daughters 'raped' their sleeping father, for Abimelech on the brink of adultery, for Leah's intercourse, for the rape of Dinah, for Reuben sleeping with his father's concubine, and four times for Potiphar's wife demanding fornication from Joseph (Gen 19:32-25; 26:10; 30:16; 24:2,7; 35:22; 39:7-14). Only three times in Genesis is the signified 'lying down' meant as holy (Gen 19:4; 28:13; 47:30).

The stages of Jesus' Mission are represented by various garments given to Joseph which are mentioned repeatedly, so often in fact that they draw the reader's attention.[76] At the beginning, his father gave him a precious *"tunic, woven of many colours"*; after this he was reduced to wearing a slave's *"garment"* — even this was stripped from him — and finally, after his ordeals pharaoh gave him a *"robe of silk"*.[77] These three garments indicate the itinerary of the Son of God. The magnificent *"coat of divers colours"* given by his father symbolises the Son's eternal glory: *"And now glorify Thou Me, O Father, with Thyself, with the glory which I had with Thee before the world was"* (Jn 17:5 DRB). Then with the Incarnation He *"emptied Himself, taking the form of a servant, being made in the likeness of men, and in habit found as a man"* (Phil 2:7 DRB). This garment, His Sacred Humanity, He even surrendered like Joseph into the hands of His accusers (Gen 39:13-15). But from hell He took His Humanity up again, as Joseph began his ascent from prison (Gen 39:21), so that finally His Risen Humanity sits at the Right Hand of the Father, there putting on the *"silk robe"* of incorruptible glory.[78]

The three garments are bound up with three pairs of dreams. Immediately after receiving his diversely coloured tunic, we hear Joseph *"recounted the vision of a dream to his brothers"* and *"he saw another dream"* (Gen 37:5,9). Then after his servant garment was taken from him, two of pharaoh's stewards related their dreams in prison (Gen 40). Two years later, pharaoh himself *"saw*

---

[76] Abbé Alban Cras, FSSP, *La symbolique du vêtement dans la Bible*, p.62.

[77] Gen 37:3; 39:12-13; 41:42.

[78] A fourth set of garments mentioned may represent the glory which clothes the saints in Heaven — see Gen 45:20-23.

a dream... slept again, and he saw another dream" (Gen 41:1,5). Joseph alone could give the meaning of all these dreams, saying, *"Doesn't interpretation belong to God? Recount for me what you have seen"* (Gen 41:8). Reading of 'dreams' may make us think of 'sleep', and perhaps the Crucifixion. Indeed, considering the content of the three sets of double dreams sequentially, they point variously to the Passion of Christ.

Jesus Christ recapitulated the whole universe by 'falling asleep', that is by dying on the Cross and rising. Joseph's two dreams show him being worshipped on earth and in heaven:

> *my sheaf seemed to rise up and stand, and your sheaves, standing in a circle, reverenced my sheaf* and *I saw by a dream, as if the sun, and the moon, and eleven stars were reverencing me.* (Gen 37:7,9)

The ultimate meaning of Joseph's dreams is that through His 'sleep', Jesus Christ — whom Joseph so richly prefigures — will be reverenced as Lord of Earth and Heaven.

From prison Joseph interpreted other men's dreams (Gen 40). These were an insoluble puzzle to everyone else. But Joseph could see that these strange dreams held men's destinies: the butler's unto his redemption; the baker's unto his condemnation. Do our dreams carry meaning? Most dreams do not, but they can. So also our lives are often insubstantial and incoherent, that is meaningless. But the ultimate meaning, what our lives add up to, is declared by the Judge Jesus, unto salvation and glory or damnation and death. The butler was faithful, and lived, indeed he was elevated from prison to a position of glory; but the baker was careless and let the birds steal the bread, and for being unfaithful, he was executed.

Do these consequences sound disproportionate? We should not be thinking so much of pharaoh's 'butler and baker' but of his *"cupbearer / chief of wine"* (ἀρχιοινοχόος) and *"miller of grain / chief of wheat"* (ἀρχισιτοποιὸς) (Gen 40:1). In Christ this is eucharistic. Their dreams are comparable to the real meaning of their lives, arising from their deepest, most hidden, mysterious thoughts (sometimes our acts of will are hidden even from ourselves and we do not know why we chose one path rather than another). But nothing is hidden from the Just Judge. The servant who is profoundly faithful to the Holy Eucharist, prefigured by the wine, is restored (ἀποκατασταθῆναι Gen 40:13; 41:13). The one who is unfaithful in handling the King's bread is hung on a gibbet of wood (κρεμασθῆναι Gen 40:19; 41:13). The message is just. Though we will be judged according to how we treated Jesus in the hungry, sick and imprisoned (Mt 25:31-46), St Paul adds it will be done to us according as we treat Jesus in the Holy Eucharist (1 Cor 11:26-32).

Joseph says *"Only remember me, when it will be well with you"* (Gen 40:14), which suggests *"Do this in memory of Me"* (Lk 22:19): assist at Holy Mass. More generally our final judgement hangs on our participation in the Passion of Christ: if when we fall asleep Jesus sees our lives have, through fear of the Lord, been sacrificial, loving, we are saved. If we have been careless, heedless of God and neighbour, we are damned.

Lest there be any doubt this is about Heaven and hell, we read that Joseph's judgements were fulfilled on *"the third day"*, which was Pharaoh's birthday, where *"he made a great feast for his servants"* (Gen 40:20), signifying the Heavenly Banquet. The word for 'servants' (עֲבָדָיו) is the same as that used for God's servants in Dt 6:13 and Is 56:6, which refers to the worship owed exclusively to God.[79] Now pharaoh stands for the Most Holy Trinity as only he is more powerful than Joseph (*"only in the kingly throne will I be above thee"* Gen 41:40), while Joseph stands here for Jesus Christ as Judge in His Sacred Humanity. Pharaoh (God) summons his servants to be brought up from prison (death) either to be restored and granted a place at the celebratory banquet (Heaven), or to be executed and *"the birds will tear your flesh"* (Gen 40:19 — which means to be tormented by the devils in hell). The destiny of each soul is declared by Joseph (Jesus), who interprets (judges) their dreams (the ultimate meaning of their inner life).

What then of pharaoh's two dreams, of seven emaciated cows devouring seven stout beauties, and then the beauty of seven, well-formed ears of grain being devoured by seven thin and blighted ones, yet in both cases the evil not gaining the form of the good? As a preliminary observation, we are authoritatively told by Joseph that the doubling of pharaoh's dream means its prophecy is fixed, certain to happen (Gen 41:32). This indicates Joseph's destiny was also fixed by his own double dream at the beginning. But the servants' dreams were each single, not doubled. Perhaps this gives room for the dreams of the butler and baker not to be fulfilled, that is in the allegory for those in a state of grace to fall into sin again, or those heading for hell to repent and reach Heaven (Ezek 33). The result of our lives, like their dreams, is not fixed as if we did not have free will, but the sum of it is only revealed at the end.

---

[79] St Thomas, *Super Boetium de Trinitate,* Q.III a.4 s.c.7 observes that the Greek for '*servies / servimus*' in Dt 6:13; Mt 4:10; Phil 3:3 all refer to the exclusive worship due to God ('*latriae servitute*').

Meanwhile pharaoh's dreams concerned not simply individuals but the whole world. And the ultimate meaning in Christ we may say is that God's Plan for the result of human history is fixed. God's Plan succeeds. Jesus is Lord. Pharaoh's dreams mean good is prior to evil; and there is more than sufficient good to see us through the evil times. Evil will not overcome the good; it devours, but cannot assimilate the form of the good, that is life and truth.

And at the centre of all this, explaining all events before and after, is the Passion. As Joseph's life led him to be forgotten in prison, so Jesus was destined for the Cross. In that dereliction came the turnaround. As Joseph then rose to be second only to pharaoh, so Jesus ascends to the right hand of God. That the six dreams happened in sleep suggests we be mindful throughout of the Passion. The first two dreams declare Jesus is Lord of Heaven and Earth; being fixed to the Cross was His earthly enthronement. The second two dreams show that the verdict at our Judgement depends upon whether we are crucified or crucify; whether we suffer with Jesus for our neighbour or whether we crucify Jesus in our neighbour; whether we worship Him in the Holy Eucharist or blaspheme Him. And the third set of dreams announces that God's victory over the world is assured: evil attacks but cannot imitate or replace the good; there is enough good already given to see the Church through to the end no matter what evil attempts.

To summarise the point on judgement, those who were born into Egypt received their ration of bread from Joseph (cf. *"Panem nostrum quotidianum da nobis hodie"* Lk 6:3). Those from outside of Egypt had to come to beg for bread or grain. While most had only to pay the due price, the account of his brothers emphasises that people received the saving food not on their terms, but on Joseph's terms, being examined closely and tested (Gen 42-44); though Joseph desired to give them bread, he wanted them to pass the test. Thanks be to God they passed and lived. So they will come to Heaven who seek God truly.

Meanwhile, the account of the butler and baker indicates the judgement on those who are Egyptians, already of Pharaoh's household, which represents Christians. If they handle the Holy Eucharist well, they are redeemed, and they come to the heavenly banquet. If they are neglectful of the king's bread, they are condemned to death, hell. The attitudes of the two men were portrayed in dreams which they themselves did not understand but which Joseph alone could interpret. This signifies that none of us is judge of our own soul, none of us truly knows what our life adds up to; but in the end we will be shown and told by Jesus, the Just Judge. This calls for a reverential fear on our part. Yet confidence too, if we believe what we read, as the following story of Elijah's miraculous survival illustrates.

ELIJAH WOKEN BY AN ANGEL

Then Ahab reported to Jezebel all that Elijah had done, and how he had killed all the prophets with the sword. And so Jezebel sent a messenger to Elijah, saying, 'May the gods do these things [and more], if by this hour tomorrow I will not have made your life like the life of one of them.' Therefore, Elijah was afraid. And rising up, he went away to wherever his will would carry him. And he arrived in Beersheba of Judah. And he dismissed his servant there. And he continued on, into the desert, for one day's journey. And when he had arrived, and was sitting under a juniper tree, he requested for his soul that he might die. And he said: 'It is enough for me, O Lord. Take my soul. For I am no better than my fathers.' And he stretched himself out, and he slept deeply in the shadow of the juniper tree. And behold, an Angel of the Lord touched him, and said to him, 'Rise up and eat.' He looked, and behold, at his head was bread baked under ashes, and a jug of water. Then he ate and drank, and again he slept deeply. And the Angel of the Lord returned a second time, and touched him, and said to him: 'Rise up, eat. For a great journey again stands before you.' And he when he had risen up, he ate and drank. And he walked by the strength of that food for forty days and forty nights, as far as the mountain of God, Horeb.

— 1 Kngs 19:1-8

If our life be in danger for serving God, if we are so depressed we no longer care to live, God will move heaven and earth to strengthen us, so that we come through to His holy mountain.

Such is our lesson from Elijah. Fully alert now to the possibility that OT 'sleeps' point to the Passion of Christ, this account of Elijah does not disappoint in yielding profound references to Jesus' crucifixion. We find allusions to the growing hostility from the rulers, to the agony in Gethsemane, the Cross, the sleep like death, the darkness, the Resurrection and even the Ascension. Amid all these themes, Elijah's passion is most profoundly about the greatest meal given to man, the Holy Eucharist. It is this that gives us strength for the journey of life.

Elijah condemned and defeated the four hundred false prophets of Baal. For this the rulers, King Ahab and Queen Jezebel, sought to have him killed. Elijah *"was afraid"*; he *"dismissed his servant"* in one place, while he *"continued on"* then prayed *"that he might die"* (1 Kngs 19:3-4). We may think of Jesus in Gethsemane stationing His Apostles before continuing on alone and preparing His Soul, according to God's Will, for death.

Then *"he stretched himself out, and he slept deeply in the shadow of the juniper tree"* (1 Kngs 19:5). That *"he stretched himself out"* images Jesus stretched out on the Cross. That *"he slept deeply in the shadow of the juniper tree"* introduces our motif of sleep, here in the shadow — indicating the gloom of Calvary, the darkened day (Mt 27:45) — of a tree: evidently the Cross. The *"juniper tree"*, or broom tree, can serve as fuel for warmth in the wilderness, but does not itself offer food for sustenance (cf. Job 30:4; Ps 119:4). But God provides.

While satanic Jezebel sends a messenger (מַלְאָךְ) to say Elijah must die, God sends His angel (same word: מַלְאָךְ), even His Son, to bring life (1 Kngs 19:2,5; Lk 22:43). The Angel of the Lord touches the sleeping Elijah, figuring Christ's divinity reunited with His Sacred Humanity, and instructs him: *"Rise up and eat"*.

"Rise" (קוּם, ἀνίστημι) as in the Resurrection; and we recall Jesus, after raising the little girl from death, then instructed *"give her something to eat"* (Mk 5:43), and after His own Resurrection also asked for something to eat.[80] If this interpretation is not yet convincing, what follows is so surely concerned with the Holy Eucharist, the fruit of the Cross, that it should leave no doubt.

On waking Elijah found *"bread baked under ashes, and a jug of water"* (1 Kngs 19:6). The phrase *"baked under ashes"* (רְצָפִים) or *"baked on hot stones"* (RSVCE) or *"hearth cake"* (DRB) is derived from that used for glowing stones, the live coals with which the seraphim purified Isaiah's lips and soul (Is 6:6), as also for the paving of the heavenly Temple in Ezekiel's vision (Ezek 40). The word for *"cakes of bread"* (עֻגָה) appears exactly seven times in the OT with a cumulative connotation unmistakably eucharistic: the cakes which Abraham offered to the Holy Trinity (Gen 18:6); the unleavened bread for the Passover meal (Ex 12:39); the manna in the desert, also for a journey to Mount Horeb (Num 11:8); the inexhaustible sustenance Elijah miraculously provided for the widow's whole household to survive the drought (1 Kngs 17:13-15); Elijah's bread of angels (1 Kngs 19:5-6); Ezekiel's 'crucifixion' food (Ezek 4:12); and wayward Ephraim symbolising unconverted souls, bread not turned, burnt black and ruined (Hos 7:8).

The *"jug"* (צַפַּחַת) of water also appears seven times in the OT: once here; three times for the miraculously inexhaustible jar of flour Elijah provided for the widow's household during the deadly drought (1 Kngs 17:12,14,16); and three times, as we have just heard, for the vessel of water at Saul's head while he slept and

---

[80] Lk 24:41 cf. Jn 21:5; Lk 24:30; Mk 16:14.

escaped death (1 Sam 26:11,12,16). Seven mentions of the *"cakes of bread"*, and seven mentions of the *"jug"* of water, and this at the 'Well of Seven' (Beersheba)[81] — shall we not think of the seven sacraments, especially of Baptism ('jug of water') and the Holy Eucharist ('cakes of bread'), which mystically issued from Jesus' pierced Heart on Calvary? It is sustenance for the journey of life provided by the Angel of the Lord, the Son of God.

Why are we told Elijah slept twice, was twice woken by the Angel, twice ate and drank (1 Kngs 19:5-8)? It shows us how troubled was his heart, how prostrated he was with exhaustion, that again we may wonder at the Passion. Or perhaps because the shadow is in the Old Covenant and the image in the New Covenant, a repeating? Or perhaps the first time representing Jesus, Our Head, Who accomplished all; and the second time representing His Body, the Church, who takes up her cross to follow Him in all? In any case, the whole is disguised in language of stark simplicity:

וַיָּקָם וַיֹּאכַל וַיִּשְׁתֶּה וַיֵּלֶךְ בְּכֹחַ הָאֲכִילָה הַהִיא
אַרְבָּעִים יוֹם וְאַרְבָּעִים לַיְלָה עַד הַר הָאֱלֹהִים חֹרֵב :

And he rose, and he ate, and he drank, and he went in strength of that food forty days and forty nights unto the mountain of the Lord at Horeb

(1 Kngs 19:8)

Each clause contains a world of meaning! Resurrection. Holy Eucharist. Most Precious Blood. Life of grace cooperating with nature. The highs and the lows in the life of Faith. Arrival at the gates of Heaven.

---

[81] Beersheba means 'Well of Seven' or 'Well of the Oath' (see Gen 21:28-33).

As Jesus spent forty days from His Resurrection until His Ascension, so Elijah spent forty days from his being touched by an angel to awake from deep sleep until arriving at the mountain where he went up to be with God (1 Kngs 19:11-13). The journey from Beersheba to Mount Horeb is about 280 miles, which for a journey of forty days requires seven miles a day, as the Church draws daily on the seven Sacraments. It is heavenly nourishment to sustain us through the wilderness until we come to the mountain of the Lord: first Jesus Christ; then His Body, the Church. All this the Church invites us to ponder, singing on the Solemnity of *Corpus Christi:*

> **R.** Elijah looked, and, behold, there was a cake baken on the coals at his head, and he arose, and did eat and drink; And went in the strength of that meat unto the mount of God.

> **V.** If any man eat of this Bread, he shall live for ever.

> **R.** And went in the strength of that meat unto the mount of God. Glory be to the Father, and to the Son, and to the Holy Ghost.

> **R.** And went in the strength of that meat unto the mount of God.[82]

---

[82] Solemnity of Corpus Christi, Matins, *Responsorium* III.

LOT AS SLEEPING VICTIM

And Lot ascended from Zoar, and he stayed on the mountain... and he dwelt in a cave, he and his two daughters with him. And the elder said to the younger: 'Our father is old, and no man remains in the land who can enter to us according to the custom of the whole world. Come, let us inebriate him with wine, and let us sleep with him, so that we may be able to preserve offspring from our father.' And so they gave their father wine to drink that night. And the elder went in, and she slept with her father. But he did not perceive it, neither when his daughter lay down, nor when she rose up. Likewise, the next day, the elder said to the younger: 'Behold, yesterday I slept with my father, let us give him wine to drink yet again this night, and you will sleep with him, so that we may save offspring from our father.' And then they gave their father wine to drink that night also, and the younger daughter went in, and slept with him. And not even then did he perceive when she lay down, or when she rose up. Therefore, the two daughters of Lot conceived by their father. And the elder gave birth to a son, and she called his name Moab. He is the father of the Moabites, even to the present day. Likewise, the younger gave birth to a son, and she called his name Ammon, that is, 'the son of my people.' He is the father of the Ammonites, even today.

— Gen 19:30-38

The following section makes uncomfortable reading. But the difficult passages of Scripture may yield the brightest light, if we do not shy away from finding meaning in them.[83] Still, I am not sure of the interpretation offered below. The Church Fathers often wrote that their reader was free to accept or reject their understanding of the spiritual sense of Scripture, offering it anyway in case it were helpful, and remaining open to a better understanding being found. Much less do I insist on my interpretations, especially not this one. But the events recorded in Gen 19 are so bizarre that they must carry a deeper meaning. Perhaps it means that those who take the Holy Eucharist unworthily will be afterwards condemned?

Lot was a relative of Abraham, but not a son, and he is not covered with glory in Genesis. He got himself captured, necessitating battle for Abraham; he was slow to leave Sodom, and then did not wish to go far away; and while Abraham inherited the Promised Land, Lot freely chose the other inheritance, which is rather foreboding, given the Promised Land represents heaven. Still, Lot himself is counted just (2 Pet 2:7).

Recalling Noah's drunken sleep as a figure of the Passion, might Lot's drunken sleep have some connection too? If so, it

---

[83] Paolo Prosperi, *Toward a Renewal of Typological Exegesis* in *Communio 37* (Fall 2010), p.418 "In this way, we also rediscover the value of a principle that, for Origen as for Jewish exegesis, was fundamental: precisely the 'difficulties' present in the biblical texts are to be understood as the place where we must seek deeper 'mysteries.' When they are placed side by side with their 'fulfillment' and with other 'figures,' the most disturbing 'figures' receive new meaning, revealing all their anagogical potential. Nothing is more impoverishing than an apparently reasonable 'selective reading' which, in the name of doing away with anthropomorphisms, is, precisely, overly human. Of course it is true that to speak of the paschal mystery is always and only to speak of the revelation of Love. But this is precisely the problem: 'This is what we don't know at the outset: what is love? In every typological exegesis, our certainties need to be submerged in the bath of enigma; they never emerge the same as before'."

does not seem to be a happy one. Lot's daughters, desperate to follow *"the custom of the whole world"*, united with their father without his willing engagement, making him so drunk that he did not wake despite the intrusive abuse. The resulting descendants were cursed:

> *Because of this, as I live, says the Lord of hosts, the God of Israel, Moab will be like Sodom, and the sons of Ammon like Gomorrah, like the dryness of thorns, and piles of salt, and a desert, all the way to eternity. The remnant of my people will despoil them, and the residue of my nation will possess them. This will come upon them for their arrogance, because they have blasphemed and have been magnified over the people of the Lord of hosts. The Lord will be a horror over them, and he will reduce all the gods of the earth.* (Zeph 2:9-11)

This unsavoury episode in the cave might signify calling on preternatural powers by making offerings in a manner unpleasing to God, in the worst cases black masses offered with stolen Hosts. Much more commonly, it signifies sacrilegious Communions, that is, those who receive the Holy Eucharist while not in a state of grace.[84] Some of the most notorious examples in our day include abortionists and the politicians who legislate to enable them; unrepentant 'men of Sodom' and those who promote 'pride' events; those living in adultery and the priests who turn a blind

---

[84] *"And my bread, which I gave to you, the fine flour, and the oil, and the honey, by which I nourished you, you placed in their sight as a sweet fragrance. And so it was done, says the Lord God. And you took your sons and your daughters, whom you bore for me, and you immolated them to be devoured. Is your fornication a small matter?"* (Ezek 16:19-20)

eye to all this. All such Communions force a 'union' with God's Body yet without a union of soul or spirit. All result in condemnation. Pope St Pius X taught:

> He who goes to Communion in mortal sin receives Jesus Christ but not His grace; moreover, he commits a sacrilege and renders himself deserving of sentence of damnation.[85]

The difference between those who end in Heaven and those who end in Hell is not that the first group did not sin, or even sin gravely, but that they repented.

When we hear of two daughters, an elder and a younger, we may think of two religions. The 'elder' might refer to the paganism of Gentiles and the 'younger' to the Mosaic rites of Jews, as paganism is the older of the two.[86] Or the 'elder' could refer to the Old Covenant and the 'younger' to the New Covenant. Applying the sisterly relation from the story, as it was the elder who corrupted the younger, we can think of Gentiles subverting Jews, or of Jews subverting Christians. Though this is not a comfortable subject, if we are willing to explore these possible interpretations, we find the Scriptures have much to say.

Examples of the first case, of Gentiles subverting Jews, include Moabite women beguiling Hebrew men into fornication and idolatry of Baal Peor, resulting in tens of thousands of deaths.[87] Or the Ammonite Queen Naamah (along with hundreds of other foreign wives) seducing King Solomon into demon worship; their

---

[85] *Catechism of Pope St Pius X*, The Blessed Eucharist, Q.37.

[86] In this account, the Septuagint uses πρεσβυτέρα for the 'elder' daughter and πρεσβύτερος (presbyter) describing Lot, which may put us in mind of priestesses and priests (Gen 19:31).

[87] Num 25:1-3; 31:16.

son Rehoboam was a disaster.[88] Or, more positively, Ezra and Nehemiah zealously expelling from the priesthood those who married foreigners, even at a time when priests were sorely needed for the rebuilding of Jerusalem and the Temple.[89] To protest this is racist completely misses the point. It is a warning against syncretism, mixing true religion with false ones. Both Ezra and Nehemiah specifically condemned the marriage of Levite priests with Ammonite and Moabite women, that is with descendants of Lot's two daughters. The point is not to say that any human being is condemned or contaminated on account of their race. Rather it is that true worship cannot mix with false; it is an abomination to share the Holy Eucharist with people who by their behaviour and dogmatic principles do not accept God's terms. The Universal Catholic Church, founded by the Son of God, can gain nothing from other religions except converts. This is the teaching of the OT and the NT.

Examples of the second case, of Judaism threatening to corrupt Christianity, abound in the NT. Judaizers brought confusion, error and strife into communities, and even sorcery was involved. Since the Middle Ages some in the Church allowed themselves to be led astray by giving too much honour to the Talmud or even falling for the Kabbalah.[90] More recently, insecure Christians caused unnecessary confusion by adopting the (unconvincing) Masoretic Psalm numbering over that of the (venerable) Septuagint and Vulgate and, much worse, Catholics have struck

---

[88] 1 Kngs 11:1-8; 14:21-26; 2 Chron 10:1-19; 12:13-14.

[89] Ezra 9:1-3; 10:6-44; Neh 13:23-31.

[90] Notably Pico della Mirandola (1463-1494), Johannes Reuchlin (1455-1522) who wrote *De arte cabalistica* (*On the Art of the Kabbalah*) in 1517, and Cardinal Giles of Viterbo (1455-1532).

the rich Gallican-monastic offertory prayers out of the Mass in favour of lamentably reduced prayers modelled on those of the synagogue. It is as if the Church wants to please man rather than God, contemning her birthright. Catholics bear their own guilt for this latter falling away. Also in the story, the younger sister cannot blame the elder; she made her own decision to listen to bad advice and copy her sister's practices.

Genesis tells us it was *"night"* when the elder daughter slept with Lot and again *"night"* when the younger daughter did the same (Gen 19:33,35). This points to the time of deepest evil, of betrayal: *"And it was night"* (Jn 13:30).

Made insensible by them, each time their father *"did not perceive it, neither when his daughter lay down, nor when she rose up"* (Gen 19:33,35). This is the privation of that relation with God of which David sings: *"Lord, thou hast proved me, and known me: Thou hast known my sitting down, and my rising up"* (Ps 138:1-2). If God does not know the daughters in this union, who does? Who are they serving? According to St Ephraim, satan boasts "to [Lot's] daughters I gave such counsels, as were pleasing to me", indicating satan inspired them.[91] The daughters did it in order to *"preserve our father's seed"* (Gen 19:32,34). satan too has seed on earth (Gen 3:15). If drunken Lot distantly represents the crucified Christ, then it seems the *"father"* here, even if not intended by the daughters, is not God but the devil, as Jesus thundered against those who falsely claim to have Abraham for a father (Jn 8:44). Recall Lot was not descended from Abraham. The daughters' successive unions represent those who offer sacrifices to God in a manner not pleasing to Him. In the

---

[91] St Ephraim, *Nisibene Hymns*, LVII.

Old Covenant this includes Aaron's sons Nadab and Abihu, for which they died (Lev 10), and King Saul, for which he lost the kingdom (1 Sam 13:9-14). In the New Covenant it is those who offer black masses, for which, if they do not repent, they are damned. In a black mass the Host is truly Christ, as Lot represents the Crucifixion; but the one to whom the offering is made is not God the Father but the father of lies.

If this is all too dark, there is a more hopeful interpretation. Let the two daughters represent Gentiles and Jews. Both were guilty for the drunken sleep of their father as both Gentiles and Jews crucified Christ.[92] Both earned death. But thanks be to God there is redemption for all who repent. So although the Moabites and Ammonites were cursed (*i.a.* Zeph 2:9-11), the Scriptures also give grounds for great hope for individual souls among them. The Ammonites win honour through their commander Achior, who knew the profound truth about Israel (Jdt 5:5-25; 13:27). Of him we read:

> *Achior, seeing the power that the God of Israel had wrought, left behind the rituals of the Gentiles. He believed in God, and he circumcised the flesh of his foreskin, and*

---

[92] Jesus laid down His life (Jn 10:18) to save the world (1 Jn 2:2; Jn 3:17; Heb 2:9), for *"all have sinned"* (Rom 3:10) and *"If we claim that we have no sin, then we are deceiving ourselves and the truth is not in us"* (1 Jn 1:8). It behooves every one of us alive today to admit that our sins are the cause of His death. Whoever with compunction asks for God's mercy will be forgiven. *"If we confess our sins, then He is faithful and just, so as to forgive us our sins and to cleanse us from all iniquity"* (1 Jn 1:9; see also 2 Chron 7:14; Prov 28:13; Is 55:7; Ezek 18:32; Lk 13:3; Acts 2:38). For further distinctions here, see St Thomas, *S.Th.* III, Q.47 a.6, where he teaches that the Romans who crucified Jesus in ignorance and the crowds of Jews who afterwards had compunction were forgiven (Lk 23:24,48), but the Jewish leaders who knowingly had the Messiah killed were not forgiven.

he was placed among the people of Israel, and so were all
the succession of his kindred, even until this present day.
(Jdt 14:6)

Meanwhile the Moabites find favour in the prophecies of
David and Jeremiah (Ps 107:10 Vg; Jer 48:47), and of course are
rehabilitated through Ruth, wife of Boaz, graced with the
staggering privilege of being in the line of mothers of the Lord
(Mt 1:5). It cannot be all bad then, to be a Moabite. There is hope
of redemption for those who were once cursed. Lot's grim story
has a silver lining.

None of this speaks against God in the slightest way. He
remains the most tender Father who wishes to feed His children
with the best of food. All are invited to become His children, but
the Holy Eucharist may only be received according to His Will,
for His Will is Love, and to reject His Will is to reject Love. The
humble will live, the proud will starve. On the Feast of *Corpus
Christi*, The Blessed Virgin Mary communicates all this in her
Magnificat, as the Church condenses it into her antiphon:

O Lord, how kindly is thy Spirit; even thine, Whose
sustenance declared thy *sweetness* unto thy children when
Thou didst send them from heaven bread tempering itself to
every man's liking. O Thou, Who hast filled the hungry with
good things, and the rich, that are proud in the imagination
of their hearts, Thou hast sent empty away.[93]

---

[93] Solemnity of Corpus Christi, Magnificat Antiphon, 1st Vespers.

Ezekiel Faces Jerusalem

And as for you, son of man, take up for yourself a tablet, and you shall set it before you. And you shall draw upon it the city of Jerusalem. And you shall set up a blockade against it, and you shall build fortifications, and you shall put together a rampart, and you shall encamp opposite it, and you shall place battering rams around it. And you shall take up for yourself an iron pan, and place it as an iron wall between you and the city. And harden your face against it, and it shall be under a siege, and you shall surround it. This is a sign to the house of Israel. And you shall sleep on your left side. And you shall place the iniquities of the house of Israel on it by the number of days that you will sleep on it. And you shall take upon yourself their iniquity. For I have given to you the years of their iniquity, by the number of the days: three hundred and ninety days. And you shall bear the iniquity of the house of Israel. And when you will have completed this, you shall sleep a second time, on your right side, and you shall assume the iniquity of the house of Judah for forty days: one day for each year; one day, I say, for each year, have I given to you. And you shall turn your face toward the siege of Jerusalem, and your arm shall be extended. And you shall prophesy against it. Behold, I have surrounded you with chains. And you shall not turn yourself from one side to the other side, until you have completed the days of your siege. And you shall take for yourself wheat, and barley...

— Ezek 4:1-9

The Passion of Christ is so harrowing that it naturally draws our attention. If we do not have hearts of stone, Christ crucified, the silent lamb, draws our sympathy. As we learn why it happened — to expiate our sins — it should provoke our repentance. For those who are moved to gratitude, to love, to imitation, the Cross is salvation. Those who prefer to ignore it, to dismiss it or explain it away, demonstrate the hardness of their hearts and will be without excuse on Judgement Day. This aspect of the Passion, as a call to repentance, is highlighted by the priest-in-exile Ezekiel.

Many prophets spoke of the Passion of Christ and exhibited it in their lives by their actions. Ezekiel endured a harrowing 'crucifixion' in anticipation of Christ. God tasked him to give a sign by sleeping (Ezek 4:4,6,9) first on his left side, then on his right side, both times bound down with bands so he could not turn from one side to the other, and thereby he would *"bear the iniquity of the house of Israel [and] Judah"* (Ezek 4:5-6), anticipating Christ, the Man of Sorrows, Who *"hath borne our infirmities and carried our sorrows"* (Is 53:4). We are told his face should be turned toward Jerusalem and his *"arm shall be extended"* (Ezek 4:7). Evidently this is an image of the Crucifixion.

The passage begins using Jesus' favoured title for Himself: *"And as for you, son of man"* (Ezek 4:1). The phrase *"son of man"* appears over ninety times in Ezekiel, but just thirty times in the rest of the OT. The same phrase appears in the NT over eighty times, often Jesus applying the title to Himself. Such emphasis, as we are all descendants of man, would be utterly redundant except it come from the Son of God, He Who came not to overpower us with His glory but to confirm us with His solidarity.[94] He became man like us to bear our iniquities, to suffer for our sins. God cannot suffer. But God assumed human nature so the Son of God could suffer among us, for us. The discomfort which Ezekiel underwent to prefigure this is something extraordinary. Imagine being pinned down at night in one position for over a year:

> *And you shall sleep on your left side... And you shall take upon yourself their iniquity. For I have given to you the years of their iniquity, by the number of the days: three hundred and ninety days. And you shall bear the iniquity of the house of Israel.* (Ezek 4:4-5)

Now the Sign of the Cross has been held up for inspection by the world not merely for 390 days, or 430 days, but almost 2,000 years. God is patient. Those who reject Him cannot say they have not been called, not been warned.

As Ezekiel lived far from Israel in Babylonian exile, God instructs him to draw a figure of Jerusalem on a tablet and his ordeal takes place beside it. So God makes him a figure of Jesus' Crucifixion outside Jerusalem. Further Ezekiel is to build models of siege works and ramparts set against his drawing of Jerusalem, the description of which echoes Jesus' lament over the city's enemies surrounding and destroying her (Lk 19:43-44; 20:21).

Worse, Ezekiel was told to take an *"iron pan, and place it as an iron wall between you and the city. And harden your face against it"* (Ezek 4:3). This indicates the relentless firmness of this prophecy, of sure punishment where there is no repentance. Ezekiel's very name means 'God strengthens' or 'God hardens'.

---

[94] Another OT phrase which Ezekiel appropriates (90% of its 30 usages) is: *"and you shall know that I am the Lord"*. This too refers to Jesus.

So God strengthens those who love Him, but hardens His Face against those who reject Him.

The *"iron pan"* is the utensil, otherwise mentioned only in Leviticus and Chronicles, used for preparing cereal offerings for the Lord.[95] Jerusalem refused to make this offering in purity. So the *"bread baked in ashes"* which Ezekiel should eat, using that same eucharistic term we remember for the saving, angelic bread given to Elijah (1 Kngs 19:6 — עֻגָה), was here turned foul. The prophet is told to *"cover it, in their sight, with the dung that goes out of a man"* (Ezek 4:12). This signifies that the Gentiles will profane Jerusalem and disperse the inhabitants: *"So shall the sons of Israel eat their bread, polluted among the Gentiles, to whom I will cast them out"* (Ezek 4:13). Ezekiel protested, and God relented: *"Behold, I have given to you cow manure in place of human dung, and you shall make your bread with it"* (Ezek 4:15). Yet the Scriptures stand today with the full warning to the whole world: repent, or eat shit. Perverse if we balk at the language but not at the fact.

Still, God is merciful and reduces our punishment upon the pleading of His holy ones. He does not remove the punishment entirely, since His mercy is just. We recall the *"iron pan"*, which because of the hardness of men's hearts evokes a similar hardness from God:

> *you shall sleep a second time, on your right side, and you shall assume the iniquity of the house of Judah for forty days: one day for each year; one day, I say, for each year, have I given to you.* (Ezek 4:6)

---

[95] Lev 2:5; 6:21; 7:9; 1 Chron 23:29.

And it was for forty years, a generation, that the Jews of Jerusalem had the chance to escape calamity by turning from the Old Law to the New, from shadow to substance, so patient is God.[96] Those who refused were seen to lose everything when the Romans laid a fearful siege and destroyed the Temple in AD 70. When the measure of sins is full, God's patience reaches its limit. Whoever denies this contradicts SS Peter and Paul (2 Pet 3:8-10; Rom 2:4-5; Gal 6:7; Heb 10:26-31).

Even so, this is not the last word. The term used for the *"chains"* (עֲבֹת Ezek 4:8), or bands, or cords, fixing Ezekiel in place, is the same used for those binding the ephod to the breastplate over the heart of the high priest (Ex 28:14*ff*); and also the ropes which could not contain Samson even as the power of God cannot be contained (Jdg 15:14; 16:12); and moreover the *"bands of love"* by which God draws the unfaithful back to Himself (Hos 11:4). These connections offer food for rumination. After all, it was not principally nails which fixed Christ to the Cross, but *"bands of love"*. It is because He loved us that He willingly bore the nails. The nails then become holy, sanctified by His Blood, by His love for us. "O sweet wood! O sweet nails! That bore His sweet weight!"[97] And because Ezekiel loved God above all, he transcends his material bands like Samson breaks ropes, by saying with willing love: *"I have been nailed to the Cross with Christ"* (Gal 2:19). This love God offers to man, draws us to Him when we offer the same in return.

This is God's Offer, why He was nailed to the Cross: His Self-Sacrifice evokes our repentance; His determined expiation allows

---

[96] See St Augustine, *Epistle LXXXII*, 2, 20.

[97] Solemnity of the Exaltation of the Holy Cross, Alleluia, *"Dulce lignum, dulces clavos, Dulcia ferens pondera"*.

our redemption; His sweetest gift is to permit our imitation. Ezekiel was a Kohen, a priest of the line of Aaron, the first High Priest. But living far from Jerusalem he could never engage in the Temple service. Still he could communicate the truth of the Cross, for this fills all time, all space, all open minds, all hearts not made of stone.

THE GOODS

OF THE CROSS

The Passion of Christ — or for simplicity, the Cross — contains so much hidden richness that it takes many great lives through many long centuries to announce worthily its fullness. At the Transfiguration, Moses and Elijah spoke with Jesus about *"His departure"*, in Greek His ἔξοδος (exodus), which signifies His Passion. The conversation doubtless included His Resurrection and Ascension given that they spoke in a cloud of glory with the transfigured Christ (Lk 9:29-35). This NT event supports the claim to find the Passion of Christ prefigured in the lives of Moses and Elijah, and more widely in that which they represent, the Law and the Prophets. The Cross stands outside of time as well as within, being from eternity central to God's Plan. Let us review the abundance of goods layered into the instrument of our redemption.

Through the Cross, God turns death into life. Adam fell asleep in order that a bride could be made from him, symbolising the

Church, 'Mother of all the living'. Noah's sleep shows that reverence for the Cross wins blessings in this life and the next. Abraham's deep sleep shows that God offers everlasting (increasing) life to those who have faith in the New Covenant. In his sleep Jacob saw the way to Heaven is the Cross, the foot of which we find at the altar in the House of God, the Church.

Approaching the Cross we find our Mother. Abimelech attests that if we respect the natural law, we will be ideally disposed for God to reveal deeper relations established with us through Calvary. Among these relations is the spiritual motherhood of the Church through the Virgin Mary, a sweet reality indicated by Isaac's first encounter with Rebekah. Boaz being troubled in his sleep then soothed by Ruth indicates Jesus' eternal joy over Mary's participation in the Passion, she who is Co-Redemptrix with Christ.

If we desire to overcome sin or death or demons, then the Cross is our victorious battle standard. Moses on the hill overcoming all weariness consoles us that Christ is ever attentive from Heaven, tireless in invigorating His Church until the end of time when the whole warfare of life will be won. Samson's blind rage bringing down the foreign temple illustrates that the Cross is the doom of demons, the destruction of the house of hell. Jonah being cast into the sea reinforces that only Jesus' Sacrifice can atone for sin, only He can appease God's wrath, and He will do this to provoke our repentance. Saul surviving his sleep thanks to David's reverence conveys that the Cross is aimed at reconciliation — but once we see this we must pursue it without forgetting. David sang in Christ: *"Into thy hands I commit my spirit"* (Ps 30:6 DRB) so that we might learn in advance how to die, even to practise preparing our soul for death each evening before we fall asleep.

The singular event of Jesus' Passion on Calvary is continued through the centuries through the offering of the same Sacrifice in Holy Mass, though here in an unbloody (or non-violent) manner. By this means God gives us the fruit of the Tree of Life, the Body of His Son, the Holy Eucharist. Joseph as interpreter of dreams shows our Particular Judgement will be given by Christ crucified. He alone will explain the meaning of our lives. How we treated the Holy Eucharist is decisive. Elijah shows that if received on God's terms, then Holy Communion sustains us, nourishes us through this vale of tears so we may come to His holy mountain, Heaven. Lot's daughters illustrate that if we disregard God's law and profane Holy Communion then we are condemned. Ezekiel's discomfort discloses God's patience with the unrepentant has a limit. The punishment will come (2 Chron 36:16).

Each of these sixteen OT accounts related to sleep gives us an insight into a power or good of the Cross. When in life we have trials, if we have internalised the greatness of the Cross, then we find it truly carries us. The Cross not only overcomes death but turns our suffering into new life.

That God wants us to be attentive to the Cross is underscored by the frequency of these prefigurations. Of the examples we have considered, eight are found in the first book of the Bible alone, Genesis (Adam, Noah, Abraham, Lot, Abimelech, Isaac, Jacob, Joseph), plus one in Exodus (Moses), totalling nine in the Torah. The historical books provide four more, in Judges (Samson), Ruth (Boaz), 1 Samuel (Saul) and 1 Kings (Elijah). The minor prophets are represented (Jonah) as also the major prophets (Ezekiel). And the greatest of the Sapiential books, the Psalms (David).

Further examples are given in brief below (in *The Inexhaustible Word*), besides a great many foreshadowings which do not so directly involve sleep. The whole Bible is replete with anticipations of Calvary.

These things were written so that we might understand reality, to see the world as God sees it, to find the way to Heaven. It might convince us that the Cross is everywhere, in fact to be found in everybody's life. We have no grounds for fear here, for God tailors each Cross to each soul, knowing what we can bear. Their various weights cover a spectrum: Adam's deep sleep prefiguring the Passion was utterly painless; Noah was anaesthetised; Isaac was consoled; Jacob felt awe; Abimelech was put to confusion; Boaz was tipsy but troubled; Moses experienced exhaustion; Saul shame; Elijah depression; Abraham dread; David was hunted; Lot was abused; Ezekiel's trial was excruciating; Joseph suffered betrayal, false accusations, long imprisonment; Jonah's suffering we cannot begin to imagine; Samson was beaten, blinded and mocked, and died. God will not load us with more than we can bear.

We observe that it was not by their morality that men were qualified to prefigure the Passion. Abraham indeed was holy, Saul not so much. Moses was internally conformed to Christ, which is not so clear for Samson. Rather being chosen by God to prefigure His Son is a matter of His election, an ineffable honour. As God loved them so much as to award them a taste of the Cross, how can we not hunger for the same?

The Passion transforms confusing, temporal experiences to gain supernatural, eternal meaning. For example, Abraham had his own reason for calling Sarah his sister, consciously adopting this strategy to avoid being killed, surmising there were some in the region who would not demur to murder a man in order that his wife become available to marry. But unconsciously, by God's direction, Abraham's activity pointed to something very high. Though the actors involved were unaware, they were prefiguring a great mystery: Christ's relationship with the Church.

As the Passion elevates the past, it is all the more credible that it elevates the future. It suggests our lives carry much more weight than we imagine. It calls us to believe and know that life is meaningful. Like the OT figures, we do not have to understand our crosses, but certainly we have to embrace them with trust. Provided our soul is literally characterised by the Cross, a mark received through accepting God's loving Gift, a mark which the angels can see, then we need not fear the end (Apoc 7:2-4; 9:1-6).

Appreciating this, we desire to be on the Cross, or at least not to reject it when it comes. Jesus, despite pain and mockery, would not get off the Cross until after He had accomplished all:

> *the chief priests, with the scribes and ancients, mocking, said: 'He saved others; Himself He cannot save. If He be the king of Israel, let Him now come down from the Cross, and we will believe Him. He trusted in God; let Him now deliver Him if He will have Him; for He said: "I am the Son of God."'* (Mt 27:41-43 DRB)

The truth of the Cross is not superficial, but deep, buried, hidden. If we love God, we seek Him.[98] If we seek Him, we will

---

[98] Cant 3:1-4 is unmatched in expressing this.

find Him.[99] And it is a delight to find the hidden Jesus.[100] He knows this, so *"he stands beyond our wall, gazing through the windows, watching through the lattices"* (Cant 2:10), obscured but calling to our soul, desiring the unveiling — the *apocalypse*.

St Augustine writes:

> In every page of these Scriptures, while I pursue my search as a son of Adam in the sweat of my brow, Christ either openly or covertly meets and refreshes me. Where the discovery is laborious my ardour is increased, and the spoil obtained is eagerly devoured, and is hidden in my heart for my nourishment...
>
> ...the most hidden meanings are the sweetest...[101]

Elsewhere the *doctor caritatis* attests that it is love more than learning which uncovers ever more connections on a given theme within the Scriptures: "which whosoever turns the eye of love to seek it, may find most copiously scattered through all the Scriptures."[102]

St Gregory of Nyssa, after identifying a score of scriptural scenes in quick succession wherein Moses prefigures Jesus, writes that Moses' heart yearned to ascend yet higher toward the ineffable invisible:

---

[99] Mt 7:7.

[100] Is 45:3; Mt 13:44.

[101] St Augustine, *Contra Faustum*, XII, 27 et 14.

[102] St Augustine, *De Trinitate*, I, 13, 31.

Therefore, the ardent lover of beauty, although receiving what is always visible as an image of what he desires, yet longs to be filled with the very stamp of the archetype.[103]

We ascend from the visible world to the invisible God, from the literal sense of the Scriptures to the spiritual sense, from obvious goods to hidden goods. Life is never sweeter than when we discover new depths in God. The numerous types we find in the Bible enkindle flames of love, ardently impelling us to seek the One Who though invisible, beyond every created form, is represented everywhere in nature and in Scripture, both made through the *Logos*, the Word of God, so He is there to be found throughout, if we search.

If in enthusiasm we search for Christ too assiduously, might we make mistakes? Is there a danger of gazing too long at clouds and seeing forms which are not there, finding whatever we are determined to find, projections of an overactive imagination? Sometimes undoubtedly. But life is more than a gift, a warfare and a mystery: life is also a game. God hides; we seek Him. And in a game, if we take mistakes too seriously, it loses its nature as a game.

Wisdom recognises life is playful:

I was with him in composing all things. And I was delighted, throughout every day, by playing in his sight at all times, playing on the globe of the earth. And my delight was to be with the sons of men. (Prov 8:30-31)

From the beginning God wanted to be with the sons of men. He was there with Adam. Adam tried to hide from God,

---

[103] St Gregory of Nyssa, *Life of Moses,* II, 231.

159

unsuccessfully. God has hidden Himself in Adam, let us hope also 'unsuccessfully'. I mean let us hope God does not remain hidden, but is found in Adam, in many, in us.

If we believe prefigurations are true, we can go still deeper into the Passion, asking what was it that flowed from His Heart on the Cross, what was the meaning of the Blood and water?

II: What Flows from Jesus' Sacred Heart?

After they approached Jesus, when they saw that He was already dead, they did not break His legs. Instead, one of the soldiers opened His side with a lance, and immediately there went out Blood and water. And he who saw this has offered testimony, and his testimony is true. And he knows that he speaks the truth, so that you also may believe. For these things happened so that the Scripture would be fulfilled: 'You shall not break a bone of Him.' And again, another Scripture says: 'They shall look upon Him, whom they have pierced.'

— Jn 19:33-37

Why was Jesus' Heart pierced with a spear after He died? It was the apogee of revelation. In the piercing of His Heart, the veil was split in the Temple, opening the Holy of Holies:

Then Jesus, crying out again with a loud voice, gave up His life. And behold, the veil of the temple was torn into two parts, from top to bottom. And the earth was shaken, and the rocks were split apart. And the tombs were opened. (Mt 27:50-52)

Prior to this, only the High Priest could enter the Holy of Holies, and that but once per year. What was there? The presence of God on the mercy seat, riding on the wings of the cherubim. But Jesus' Heart is the real Holy of Holies, not made with human hands. He had come to show us the Father. And now this was revealed. By His most profound sleep, His death, by the piercing of His Heart, Jesus showed how much the Father loves us: enough to give us His Only Begotten Son. As the human will of Jesus was perfectly conformed to the Divine Will, the human love of Jesus perfectly reveals the divine love the Father, Son and Spirit hold toward us.

Significantly, it was not the opening of His Heart which caused Jesus' death, but His death which opened, or revealed, His Heart. That is to say, it is the fact that He died for us, even praying His executioners be forgiven, which reveals how absolute and prodigious is this Love for us. What more could He do?

In the seventeenth century, St Margaret Mary Alacoque, hidden in the cloister, wrote that from Jesus' Sacred Heart flows mercy for sinners, charity for those seeking perfection, and love and light for those already friends with God and who wish to advance His glory. One who advanced to this glory was the Servant of God, Madame Elisabeth of France, martyred at the guillotine in 1794. She overcame the French Revolution forever, having peacefully prayed the following:

Adorable Heart of Jesus, in recognition of Your infinite charity, I give You my heart, and with it, all that I have in this world, all that I am, all that I will do, all that I will suffer. But, finally, my God, I pray You, may this heart not be unworthy of You; make it like unto Yours, surround it with Your thorns, closing it to all wrong affections; establish Your Cross within it; may it feel its price, may it savour its delights; fill it with Your Divine flames.

What kind of love arouses a desire to give all to the Beloved, including our sufferings, to accept thorns, and go serenely to a cruel death?[104] The OT helps us find answers, helps us to understand the nature of the Sacred Heart. In the following five sections, fitting for the Five Wounds Jesus wore on the Cross, we see first He loves the whole Church as His Bride. Then He loves each individual Saint composing the Church. Thirdly, His Heart, produces the Sacraments, which we ought to love as we love, Him. Fourth, the form of His Heart is Wisdom, in it we taste the highest truths to which a mortal soul can attain. And fifth, His Heart pours out life-giving grace.

We find these five layers by first revisiting the deep sleep of Adam, then considering Noah's ark. The third is found in the service of the Levitical priests, descendants of Levi, whose name comes from לֵב , 'lev', meaning heart, mind or inner man. Hence the Book of Leviticus is the heart of the Torah, the middle one of the Five Books of Moses. Next we meditate on Samson killing a lion and lastly on Ezekiel's most famous vision.

---

[104] The meekness, forgiving spirit and even humour of countless martyrs testifies to this supernatural love.

HIS BRIDE, THE CHURCH

And so the Lord God sent a deep sleep upon Adam. And when he was fast asleep, he took one of his ribs, and he completed it with flesh for it. And the Lord God built up the rib, which he took from Adam, into a woman. And he led her to Adam. And Adam said: 'Now this is bone from my bones, and flesh from my flesh. This one shall be called woman, because she was taken from man.'

— Gen 2:21-23

We have seen that Adam's *"deep sleep"* prefigures Christ's crucifixion, and the generation of Eve from Adam's side bespeaks the issuing of the Church from Jesus' side. St Augustine teaches:

As a wife was made for Adam from his side while he slept, the Church becomes the property of her dying Saviour, by the sacrament of the Blood which flowed from His side after His death.[105]

As Eve was successively Virgin, Bride and Mother, so the Church is all these simultaneously. St John Chrysostom preaches that it is from that which flowed from Christ's side that the Church consists.[106]

How is this? Because as it is from Adam's living substance that Eve grew, the Church grows from the living substance of the Son

---

[105] St Augustine, *Contra Faustum*, XII, 8.

[106] St John Chrysostom, *Homily* LXXXV.

of God: the Holy Eucharist.[107] We eat the Body of Christ to become One Body with Christ.

In case we still do not see it, Sacred Scripture contains numerous connections. The first Adam, because of his sin, could not eat from the *"tree of life"* (Gen 2:9; 3:22-24). But Jesus, the New Adam, hung *"upon a tree"* (Acts 5:30) so that we can be nourished now by His Body, which is the fruit of Mary's womb, the Divine Fruit hanging on the true Tree of Life, the Cross. At first God told Adam: *"you shall not eat"* lest *"you die a death,"* (Gen 2:17); but the banquet prepared, the Son of God says: *"Take and eat. This is My Body"* (Mt 26:26) for *"whoever eats My Flesh and drinks My Blood has eternal life"* (Jn 6:55).

This conforms us to Christ, this makes us like God, so the serpent might eventually have bitten his tongue after whispering what he thought was a lie but which turned out, like Caiaphas' prophecy (Jn 11:51), to be more deeply true than he could ever guess: *"God knows that, on whatever day you will eat from it... you will be like gods"* (Gen 3:5). What a happy fault of Adam, for however *"good to eat, and beautiful to the eyes, and delightful to consider"* (Gen 3:6) the fruit on Eden's Tree of Life, it is inconceivable that it be as profoundly appealing as that Fruit which God gave in the fullness of time: the Body of His Beloved Son in the Holy Eucharist.

This same link between Eden and Calvary is extolled in liturgical prayers of great rank: the Preface of the Holy Cross

---

[107] To his quote above (see footnote 105), St Augustine continues: "The woman made out of her husband's side is called Eve, or Life, and the mother of living beings; and the Lord says in the Gospel: *'Except you eat the Flesh of the Son of man, and drink His Blood, you shall not have life in you'"* (Jn 6:53 DRB).

(used from Passion Sunday to Maundy Thursday, and on feasts of the Holy Cross and the Most Precious Blood) reads:

> Who didst establish the salvation of mankind in the wood of the Cross, that from whence death came into the world, thence a new life might spring, and that he who by a tree overcame, by a tree might be overthrown: through Christ our Lord.[108]

The same motif is repeated on Good Friday in the sixth-century hymn *Pange lingua gloriosi.*[109] All these connections are to aid us if we wish to understand what was born from Christ's Sacred Heart, urging us to look to Eden. There is scarcely a clearer picture of Christ's pierced side than Eve coming from Adam.

The Church, to have divine Life, must be formed from God's own substance, or she could never rise higher than the merely human. Only the divine will do, a participation in the uncreated; nothing created suffices. So there was no more fitting way for Eve to be formed than from Adam, because this images God's prior intention that the Church come from His Incarnate Son. Moreover, Jesus loves the Church so much that He desires to live in her (Jn 14:20; 17:21). Love is a reciprocal but non-symmetrical cycle. Eve came from Adam; then Adam cleaves to Eve; and new life is conceived, later to be born. So Creation came from God (that is not materially, but through His understanding and power); then God enters creation; and new life, the Church, is conceived,

---

[108] *Qui salutem humani generis in ligno Crucis constituisti: ut, unde mors oriebatur, inde vita resurgeret: et, qui in ligno vincebat, in ligno quoque vinceretur: per Christum Dominum nostrum.*

[109] Composed by Venantius Fortunatus (✝609).

166

to be born bodily into Heaven at the end of time. Adam and Eve show us this outline of the greatest of all Plans in their bodies.

The specific use of Adam's rib with its flesh was not an arbitrary decision by God. The Church comes not from Christ's Head nor from Christ's Feet, because, astonishingly, God wants to make a Bride for His Jesus who is in a sense equal to Him.[110] Not that the Church is equal to His Eternal Divinity. But, as with the Blessed Virgin Mary, she is made a companion in the work of redemption. This calls for a cooperation between the Principle, Christ, and us, His members, who willingly imitate Him, a holy concurrence that can only be achieved by grace. Thus as Adam declares Eve to be *"bone from my bones, and flesh from my flesh"*, so the Church is drawn from the Divinity and Humanity of God Incarnate, beginning temporally with His sleep on the Cross, coming from His Heart.

What further significance is associated with the rib which God extracted from Adam to fashion Eve? The inspired term used by Moses is צֵלָע (Gen 2:21-22). It is the same word used for the *"side"* of the ark of the covenant (Ex 25:12), as for the *"side"* of the Tabernacle (Ex 26:20), for the *"side"* of the altar of holocaust (Ex 27:7) and also for the *"side"* of altar of incense (Ex 30:4), for the *"side chambers"* of the Temple (1 Kngs 6:5), the *"boards"* lining the inside of the Holy Place (1 Kngs 6:15) and again the *"side chambers"* described in Ezekiel's vision of the new Temple (Ezek 41:5*ff*). In all these cases the term is used for structures which surround the ineffable, holiness, even God's presence. Ribs surround and protect the heart of man, that ineffable organ which means life, where, we hope, God dwells in us.

---

[110] St Thomas, *S.Th.* I, Q.92 a.3.

More vitally: what 'part' of God did Jesus give to begin His Church? A touch of His Divinity: spiritual, invisible, integral. God is Love. There is no 'part' of the Divinity other than pure Love Himself. Our imagination flounders not because love is illusory but because it is ultimate reality. But Adam's rib depicts it perfectly, being the closest of bones to his heart. From the love most real which poured from His Heart on Calvary, received first by His Mother Mary, the Church began. Mary is Virgin, Bride, Mother; so is the Church. Mary is His helpmate in the work of redemption of every soul; so is the Church. Jesus loves Mary above all other souls; how much, then, does He love the Church (in which Mary is included). There is literally nothing ever created which Jesus loves more than the Church, His One and Only Bride.

One consequence of this is that divorce is unthinkable. Today the financial corruption in the Roman Curia seems to be so ingrained, and conducted by men so ruthless in destroying would-be reformers, that it defeats a normal heart to hope it will be overcome. Worse still is the doctrinal confusion promoted by powerful bishops' conferences. This is certainly deliberate, albeit impossible to tell how much is from cowardice and how much from anti-Catholic malice. The liturgical desolation lies somewhere between St Peter's denial and Judas' betrayal. And there is little on earth so satanic as the sexual abuse of the vulnerable by priests, the covering up of this by bishops, and the promotion of those who cover it up by Rome. Now while all those responsible for this face hell if they fail to repent, not for one moment does it mean that Jesus will abandon His Bride.

No matter how corrupt, insane, perverse and filthy members of the Church become, Jesus will never divorce her. He will allure her, heal her, purify her, sanctify her so that:

He might offer her to Himself as a glorious Church, not having any spot or wrinkle or any such thing, so that she would be holy and immaculate." (Eph 5:27)

In the following sections we will glimpse how Jesus does this.

Meanwhile, if we did not know the Church is Jesus' Bride, then would we not fear being deservedly abandoned? The Protestants have turned away in disgust at her; the schismatics have done similarly. Incredibly, they imagine that they are somehow a bride more attractive to Christ, as if He would change His Heart and choose another than His first and only One. But thanks be to God, His Son knew *"from the beginning"* that He would never, never divorce (Mk 10:4-9). His love is far higher than ours (Is 55:3-13).

OMNES SANCTOS

Make yourself an ark from smoothed wood... The length of the ark shall be three hundred cubits, its width fifty cubits, and its height thirty cubits... Then you shall set the door of the ark at its side...

— Gen 6:14-16

The account of Eve being fashioned from Adam illustrates the origin of the Church as a whole from the side of Christ. A few chapters later the account of the animals departing Noah's Ark shows the members of the Church also as individuals — that is all the saints — who issue from Jesus' Sacred Heart. He loves us one and all. His love is creative. Without it we would not exist.

Writing of Christ's saving death, which we enter by Baptism, St Peter draws an analogy with the Flood:

as in the days of Noah, when the ark was being built. In that ark, a few, that is, eight souls, were saved by water. And now you also are saved, in a similar manner, by baptism... through the resurrection of Jesus Christ. (1 Pt 3:20-21)[111]

Here the ark is the instrument of salvation for those who survived the deluge, God's just punishment for sin. Later St Peter compares the Flood with the calamity prepared for the very end of the world (2 Pet 2:5). All this fits with the Book of Wisdom referring to the *"wood"* of the ark as the instrument of salvation: *"when water*

---

[111] St Ambrose, *De Officiis*, III, 18, 102-109, deepens the comparison, writing that as down came the flood waters and destroyed all life except that safe in the ark, so in Baptism (and repentance) the Holy Spirit descends and burns up all impurity in the soul, leaving only the core which is our conversation with God.

destroyed the earth, wisdom healed it again, guiding the just by means of contemptible wood" (Wis 10:4). By *"contemptible wood"*, here the Holy Spirit would have us reconsider the Cross (Dt 21:23; Gal 3:13).

The Church's greatest scholar of Scripture, St Jerome, identifies the animals on the ark with the members of the Church, suggesting the mix of sinners and saints is represented by the mix of species, *"the leopard with the kids, the wolf with the lambs"* (cf. Is 11:6).[112] And whereas Christians do turn on one another like beasts, to *"bite and devour one another"* (Gal 5:14-15), harmony must have reigned on Noah's ark, or only a few carnivores would have exited. So the presence of All Saints in Jesus' Heart allows no final divisions among us. There is no division in His Heart. If we hate a saint, any saint, then we cannot exist in Heaven. That includes all saints on earth, all who will ever get to Heaven. If we hate one of them, we damn ourselves. We must love all that are His. The Venerable Bede preached:

Never shall there be discord anywhere there, but all things in harmony. For everywhere there, things are in such concord that all the saints are at unity with each other in

---

[112] St Jerome, *Altercatio Luciferiani et Orthodoxi,* 22 "Noah's ark was a type of the Church, as the Apostle Peter says. In Noah's ark few, that is, eight souls, were saved through water: which also after a true likeness does now save us, even Baptism. As in the ark there were all kinds of animals, so also in the Church there are men of all races and characters. As in the one there was the leopard with the kids, the wolf with the lambs, so in the other there are found the righteous and sinners, that is, vessels of gold and silver with those of wood and of earth... The daylight would fail me if I were to explain all the mysteries of the ark and compare them with the Church."

one peace and joy. Everywhere there, all things are tranquil and quiet.[113]

Such harmony does not come to us easily. But the Blood which poured from Jesus' Heart works an intrinsic purification of the faithful, while the persecutions of the enemy serve as an extrinsic unifying factor:

These [the saints in Heaven] are the ones who have come out of the great tribulation, and they have washed their robes and have made them white by the blood of the Lamb. (Apoc 7:14)

St Augustine and Philo the Jew both recognise that God ordered the ark to be made with dimensions proportionate to the figure of a great man: three hundred cubits long, fifty wide, thirty high. Evidently this man is lying down. So we think of sleep, or death. With this imagery in mind, St Augustine connects the "opening" of Jesus' Heart on the Cross (Jn 19:34) with the "door" in the side of the ark (Gen 6:16):

A suggestive word was made use of by the evangelist, in not saying pierced, or wounded His side, or anything else, but *'opened';* that thereby, in a sense, the gate of life might be thrown open, from whence have flowed forth the sacraments of the Church, without which there is no entrance to the life which is the true life. That blood was shed for the remission of sins; that water it is that makes up the health-giving cup, and supplies at once the laver of baptism and water for drinking. This was announced beforehand, when Noah was

---

[113] St Bede, *Panegyric to All Saints,* Sermon XVIII.

commanded to make a door in the side of the ark, by which the animals that were not to perish by the deluge entered; which animals prefigured the Church.[114]

If we do not think of Jesus when we hear of Noah's ark, we have not understood the meaning of the story. If we do not think of His pierced Heart when we hear of the door in the ark, we have not understood the heart of the story.

The most salient lesson in Noah's apocalyptic life is how vital it is to be on the ark. While it is not obvious that one must be baptised in Christ, it is clear enough that one had to be on the ark or die. God teaches us about the things which are harder to see through the things which are easier to see; revealing to us the things which are more distant from us through the things that are closer to us; the spiritual through the material; the eternal through the historical. There is no salvation outside of the ark, Jesus Christ. But if we die with Him, if we are baptised in Him, then we may rise with Him (cf. 2 Tim 2:11).

Children are much more likely to understand the necessity of Baptism through the story of Noah's ark than through a class on sacramental theology. Therefore, caring for His children, God wrote the story into history itself. Whoever by Baptism enters through Jesus' Sacred Heart into His Body, and rests there, will survive the flood of death, finally emerging to the other side alive: Heaven (cf. Gen 8:15-19).

Twice then in Noah's life we have seen the Passion of Christ was prefigured. Once by the ark, the figure of a man sleeping, with an opening in his side through which all the saved entered and exited, depicting Jesus' Sacred Heart opened on the Cross.

---

[114] St Augustine, *In Evangelium Ioannis Tractatus*, CXX, 2 on Jn 19:31ss.

And after by Noah's drunken sleep, the reactions of his three sons showing that blessings or curses hang upon how we react to the Crucifixion. Which was a greater work for Noah, building the ark and saving the world or planting a vine and lying down drunk? We probably think the former. But in both he prefigured Christ's Passion.

So it is in the spiritual life: in the beginning it takes great effort, perhaps we want to play our part to save the world, perhaps we engage in big projects. Yet over time we find we can love more and more by 'doing' less and less, more concentrated on the essentials, on the present moment. We may reach a point where we love God in our sleep — it is our only thought as we fall asleep and when we wake up. Both prefigurations occurred in Noah's life, marking, as it were, the beginning and the end. Both are good. Perhaps it means, eventually the saints can achieve more in their sleep than all the early rising and toiling till late of the worldly (cf. Ps 126:2)? We will not know the meaning of our lives until Judgement Day. There will be lots of surprises.

SACRAMENTS

> The High Priest *completing his service at the altar, so as to*
> *magnify the offering to the Most High King, he extended his*
> *hand to make a libation, and he offered from the blood of*
> *the grape. At the base of the altar, he poured out a divine*
> *fragrance to the Most High, the King of all.*
>
> — Sir 50:15-17

The *"blood and water"* (Jn 19:34) which flowed from Jesus'
Sacred Heart on Calvary signify the Sacraments. The water stands
for Baptism, the Blood for the Holy Eucharist. By these two all
the Sacraments are indicated. Baptism is the first Sacrament, the
gateway, without which none of the others can be received. The
Holy Eucharist is the highest Sacrament toward which all others
are ordered, it being union with God. Such is the teaching of the
Angelic Doctor.[115] Such is the teaching of the Church Fathers. St
John Chrysostom says it is from this water and Blood that the
Church is born and nourished, indeed to drink from the chalice at
Holy Mass is to drink from Jesus' pierced side on the Cross.[116]

---

[115] St Thomas, *S.Th.* I, Q.92 a.3 "I answer that, It was right for the woman to be
made from a rib of man... for the sacramental signification; for from the side
of Christ sleeping on the Cross the Sacraments flowed — namely, Blood and
water — on which the Church was established."

[116] St John Chrysostom, *Homily* LXXXV on Jn 19 "For *'there came forth*
water and blood'. Not without a purpose, or by chance, did those founts come
forth, but because by means of these two together the Church consists. And the
initiated know it, being by water indeed regenerated, and nourished by the
Blood and the Flesh. Hence the Mysteries take their beginning; that when you
approach to that awful cup, you may so approach, as drinking from the very
side."

This sacramental outpouring of Blood and water on Calvary has a long history of prefiguration in the OT by the pouring out of libations, that is drink offerings, against the altar. If we think upon how long in advance and with how much earnest ceremony and with how much jubilation these prefigurations were accompanied, we are helped in understanding the centrality of the pierced Heart, of its supernatural working, of the joy it rightly produces.

We recall that immediately after Jacob dreamt of a ladder reaching Heaven, he declared the place to be the House of God (*"Beth-el"*, Gen 28:18) and anointed with oil the rock upon which he had slept. Years later he returned to this place and, in a significant development, he poured out wine too (Gen 35:7,14). The oil signified the anointing of a future altar. The wine signified the future pouring out of blood. That altar would be the Cross; the Blood would be Christ's:

> *In truth, he set up a monument of stone, in the place where*
> *God had spoken to him, pouring out libations over it, and*
> *pouring oil, and he called the name of that place, 'Bethel'.*
> (Gen 35:14-15)

If this action stood alone we could hardly make sense of it. But it would develop in scale and clarity through the centuries.

Hundreds of years after Jacob's drink offering, God commanded Moses when building the tabernacle in the desert to sanctify the altar of holocaust by pouring out libations of wine upon it for seven days. The context is thoroughly sacramental, or eucharistic, mentioning the altar, the sacrificial lamb, the cereal offering of fine flour mixed with oil, wine poured out, the holocaust, the service of the priests, and God's Presence among His People (Ex 29:37-46). Anticipating the reverence due to the

Blood and water which issued from Christ's side, the *"pitchers for pouring"* (Num 4:7) out the drink offerings in the tabernacle were made of precious metals, silver and perhaps gold. Not any Levite could touch these, but they were entrusted to the care of the Kohathites who had care of the ark of the Covenant and all the service in the inner sanctuary. For transportation these vessels would be placed on the table for the bread of presence which was first covered with a cloth of blue (signifying the Divine), along with the bread of presence itself, and these were covered with cloth of scarlet (signifying the Sacred Humanity, the Most Precious Blood) and then for further protection a goatskin — think of Jacob veiled as Esau (Gen 27:13-29), the younger disguised as the older, the New Covenant concealed in the Old.

The wine libations continued in Solomon's Temple over the altar of holocaust, and again when the Temple was rebuilt after the Babylonian exile. Poetically the Scriptures allude to the signification of wine as blood. We read of the High Priest:

> *completing his service at the altar, so as to magnify the offering to the Most High King, he extended his hand to make a libation, and he offered from the blood of the grape. At the base of the altar, he poured out a divine fragrance to the Most High, the King of all.* (Sir 50:15-17)

Ever since Noah this *"blood of the grape"* has spoken of the Most Precious Blood of Christ. So Ezekiel saw the future:

> *thus says the Lord God: 'These are the rituals of the altar, in whatever day it will be made, so that holocausts may be offered upon it, and blood may be poured out...'* (Ezek 43:18)

At some point in history, water too was poured down the side of the altar during the Feast of Tabernacles. For six days of the week-long feast, *living water was poured* together with wine libations over the victims and the altar. This detail is not mentioned in the OT, but rabbis say it was a command of the oral law. Living water means water from a spring or rain, suitable for purification, not standing or 'dead' water. Ultimately it alludes to the Holy Spirit in Baptism:

> *If you knew the gift of God and Who it is that asks you for a drink, you would have asked Him and He would have given you living water.* (Jn 4:10)

Certainly for the Feast of Tabernacles during the Second Temple period (after the Babylonian exile), the water for libations was drawn from the Pool of Siloam by priests who led the procession of pilgrims carrying their branches back to the Temple through the Water Gate located on the side of the City of David. According to the Mishnah, the ceremony was carried out with such lively rejoicing that "whoever has not witnessed the joy at the water-drawings, has never really seen joy in all his days".[117] This makes perfect sense in anticipation of Baptism. In fact the joy of the Jews is a reproach to the weak faith of Christians, when the former rejoice more over a figure than Christians rejoice over the reality.

In due course the reality came. Normally on the last day of the festivities no water was poured out. But one year, on the last great day of the feast,

---

[117] Mishnah Sukkah 5:1.

Jesus was standing and crying out, saying: 'If anyone thirsts, let him come to Me and drink: whoever believes in Me, just as Scripture says, "From his heart shall flow rivers of living water."' (Jn 7:37-38)

The Messiah had come to complete the feast, to fulfil the figure, when the water and Blood poured out from His Heart, a libation over Victim and Altar (the Cross). Here is grounds for rejoicing. The waters of Baptism cleanse us from all sin, original sin and all those we have committed as well, and it washes away all the punishment due to sin. Then the Holy Eucharist, even the Host which by concomitance contains within it the Blood, repeatedly washes our soul should it become (which is likely) marred by sin after Baptism: *"Jesus Christ... Who has loved us and has washed us from our sins with His Blood"* (Apoc 1:5).

The OT foreshadowings are hard to understand on their own. Why were they done, except that Moses commanded it so? But why did he command it so, except God spoke to him; and then the rituals make perfect sense in the light of Jesus Christ. They were always aimed at expressing the love and operation of His Son's Sacred Heart. This is a miracle of history which only God can work. The Old Law is pregnant with the New. As the hearts of many Catholics grow cold, indifferent to what Jesus poured out for us on the Cross, God can even today permit signs to emerge which ought to remind us — or others more deserving. *Breaking Israel News* reported in 2016 of a determined attempt to restore the old worship. Men enrolled as *Kohanim* processed to the Siloam Spring in Jerusalem:

at the base of the Mount Moriah, where they filled the flask with three log of spring water (approximately two pints) and returned to the Temple. Two *Kohanim* then ascended the stone altar in the Temple's inner courtyard, placing two silver cups on the southwestern corner. One *Kohen* poured the water from the silver flask while the second *Kohen* simultaneously poured wine from the second cup, both liquids flowing into holes in the altar specially prepared for this ceremony. Willow branches were arranged in the four corners of the altar. The entire ceremony was accompanied by blasts from silver trumpets.[118]

The Temple mentioned here is notional. A temporary altar was erected near but not on the Temple Mount, currently unreachable for Judaic ceremonies due to the strong presence there of the Muslims. In any case, attempted re-enactments of the Old Law cannot help proclaiming the New. Mount Moriah, where the re-enactment took place, is the locality where Jesus was crucified. The willow branches at the four corners speak of the Cross reaching to the four corners of the world (or four directions of the compass). The blasts of the trumpets mentioned are a pre-echo of those which will sound on the Last Day, when Jesus will return to Judge all, which is profoundly relevant to the re-enactments, as we will soon see. First it is worth noting that each year preparations develop, so that in 2018 it was reported:

The *Kohanim* wore vestments that were made according to Biblical standards for use in the Temple and several played long silver trumpets that had been prepared by the Temple Institute for use in the Third Temple. One *Kohen* carried a silver vessel used for the libation while the High Priest

---

[118] Israel 365 News, Report 21/10/2016.

carried a spectacular gold vessel prepared this year for this year's service. 'A vessel like this has not been seen since the Temples stood,' Rabbi Hillel Weiss, spokesman for the Sanhedrin and an organiser of the event, told *Breaking Israel News*.[119]

There are not a few Messianic Jews, Protestants and Catholics, including Church Fathers, who believe if the Temple is rebuilt in Jerusalem then it will signal the coming of the Antichrist and the Apocalypse, hence the trumpets. A striking painting belonging to the Temple Institute shows two Levitical priests pouring water and wine libations into two silver vessels fixed on the south-west corner of the altar. The liquids stream down to the base of the altar, the accompanying text explains, reaching the ground simultaneously. But if they were to look across Jerusalem, they would see Golgotha, where Jesus was crucified facing east toward the Temple. And perfectly mirroring the south-west corner of the altar, where the water and wine flowed down, is the wound on the right side of His chest, where from His Sacred Heart flowed saving water and Blood. As the Virgin Mary is the true altar of incense, so Jesus Christ is the true altar of holocaust. There is no need to rebuild it, no need to rebuild the Temple. He has already raised it up, offers the Holy Sacrifice daily in the Mass and, like His Heart, this is open to all who desire to see God's glory and who thirst for everlasting life. Perhaps all the efforts to re-enact the ancient ceremonies will be precisely the occasion for widespread conversions? In God's time at least. If man can rejoice over water and wine, how much more over Baptism and the Most Precious Blood, that is to say, over all the Sacraments.

---

[119] Israel 365 News, Report 30/9/2018.

The Maccabean Jews, that remnant of the 'end-times', knew well how to pray for their brothers in exile. They teach us too:

May God do good to you, and may he remember his covenant with Abraham and Isaac and Jacob, his faithful servants. May he give you all a heart to worship him and to do his will with a strong heart and a willing spirit. May he open your heart to his law and his commandments, and may he bring peace. May he hear your prayers and be reconciled to you, and may he not forsake you in time of evil. We are now praying for you here. (2 Macc 1:2-6)

WISDOM

Samson descended with his father and mother to Timnah. And when they had arrived at the vineyards of the town, he saw a young lion, savage and roaring, and it met him. Then the Spirit of the Lord rushed upon Samson, and he tore apart the lion, like a young goat being torn into pieces, having nothing at all in his hand. And he was not willing to reveal this to his father and mother. And he went down and spoke to the woman who had pleased his eyes. And after some days, returning to marry her, he turned aside so that he might see the carcass of the lion. And behold, there was a swarm of bees in the mouth of the lion, with a honeycomb. And when he had taken it in his hands, he ate it along the way. And arriving to his father and mother, he gave them a portion, and they also ate it. Yet he was not willing to reveal to them that he had taken the honey from the body of the lion. And so his father went down to the woman, and he made a feast for his son Samson. For so the young men were accustomed to do. And when the citizens of that place had seen him, they presented to him thirty companions to be with him. And Samson said to them: 'I will propose to you a problem, which, if you can solve it for me within the seven days of the feast, I will give you thirty shirts and the same number of tunics. But if you are not able to solve it, you shall give me thirty shirts and the same number of tunics.' And they answered him, 'Propose the problem, so that we may hear it.' And he said to them, 'Food went forth from the eater, and sweetness went forth from the strong.' And they were unable to solve the proposition for three days. And when the seventh day had arrived, they said to the wife of Samson: 'Coax your husband, and persuade him to reveal to you what the proposition means. But if you are not willing to do so, we will burn you and your father's house. Or have you called us to the wedding in order to despoil us?' And she shed tears before Samson, and she complained, saying: 'You hate me, and you do not love me. That is why you do not want to explain to me the problem, which you have proposed to the sons of my people.' But he responded: 'I was not willing to reveal it to my father and mother. And so, how can I reveal it to you?' Therefore, she wept before him during the seven days of the feast. And at length, on the seventh day, since she had been troubling him, he explained it. And immediately she revealed it to her countrymen. And they, on the seventh day, before the sun declined, said to him: 'What is sweeter than honey? And what is stronger than a lion?'

— Jdg 14:5-18

Samson's riddle says: *"Food went forth from the eater, and sweetness went forth from the strong"* (Jdg 14:14). This can be rephrased: "What flowed forth from the Sacred Heart of Jesus?" Probably this claim needs some explaining.

A lion was killed at a vineyard of Timnah. This lies in the territory of Judah, therefore we are speaking of a lion of Judah, which according to the first and last book of the Bible, indicates

Jesus (Gen 49:9-10; Apoc 5:5).[120] After the lion was killed by a wayward judge of Israel (Samson or Caiaphas), honey was drawn from its carcass. What does this mean?

The wedding guests gave a solution, which Samson acknowledged as correct, but they presented it to us also in the form of a question: *"What is sweeter than honey? And what is stronger than a lion?"* (Jdg 14:17). Honey is sweet, pure, rich and even inebriating (Cant 5:1-3). Yet there is one reality which the Bible tells us is sweeter, purer and richer than honey, even spiritually intoxicating, which answers the mystery correctly at a deeper level: wisdom.

The Sapiential Books state: *"How sweet is your eloquence to my palate, more so than honey to my mouth!"* (Ps 108:103), showing it was fitting that the bees began their work in the lion's mouth. Another inspired song sings: *"the judgments of the Lord are true, justified in themselves... sweeter than honey and the honeycomb"* (Ps 18:10-11). Wisdom herself declares: *"my spirit is sweeter than honey"* (Sir 24:27).

When Jonathan in his wartime hunger filled himself with honey, his eyes were enlightened, his countenance shone (1 Sam 14:27-29) — so one who fights evil, fasts in the body and feasts with the mind, contemplating Divine Wisdom, will be spiritually transformed.

---

[120] St Augustine and St Ephraim see Samson as prefiguring Christ and the lion as representing the devil (St Augustine, *Contra Faustum*, XII, 32; cf. 1 Pet 5:8) or death (St Ephraim, *Nativity Hymn* 8) or else indeed as Jesus (St Ephraim, *Nisibene Hymn* 39,17). The various interpretations all have value in so far as they convey truth. Typology is necessarily multivalent, as there are many more spiritual realities than there are material to represent them.

Wisdom, St Thomas teaches, is a gift both speculative (contemplation) and practical (what to do).[121] The highest speculative wisdom on earth is to know in the Spirit that the Son of God died on the Cross to redeem us from our sins; and His Sacrifice is continued in Holy Mass; whereat He is truly, really, substantially present in the Holy Eucharist. The apogee of practical wisdom is to receive Holy Communion worthily, with a self-sacrificial love which fills all our days.

The reason belief in the Holy Eucharist is the apogee of wisdom is because it is the ultimate mystery which entails all others. First it is the fruit of Holy Mass, the living memorial of Christ's Passion, Resurrection and Ascension. Further the Mass could never have been instituted without the Incarnation. Next the Incarnation depends upon the work of the Blessed Trinity and the assent of the Blessed Virgin Mary. Further the Holy Eucharist is made present among us through the Church, through the priesthood, for our redemption. This in turn makes sense of Creation and God permitting the Fall. It is all aimed at the Communion of Communions in Heaven. To hold all this in one's head, or better to preach it, is truly *"sweeter than honey"* in the mouth. It is Wisdom.

St Thomas observes "wisdom may be described as 'sweet-tasting science'", suggesting the mind discerns spiritual pleasure in wisdom as the palate enjoys sugary sweetness in tasting.[122] Indeed the two concepts share the same etymological root: *'sapere',* which means to be wise as well as to taste. Now the best

---

[121] St Thomas, *S.Th.* II-II, Q.45 a.3.

[122] St Thomas, *S.Th.* II-II, Q.45 a.2 ob.2 *"sapientia quasi sapida scientia"* (cf. Sir 6:23). Wisdom *"will feed him with the bread of life and understanding. And she will give him to drink from the water of salvific wisdom"* (Sir 15:3).

reality we can 'taste' is God Himself: *"O taste, and see that the Lord is sweet"* (Ps 33:9 DRB). We have no greater help on earth for receiving the Gift of wisdom, sweet union with God, than Holy Communion, "having within it all sweetness".[123] In this light, we better understand what Moses wrote: *"And the house of Israel called its name 'Manna.' It was like white coriander seed, and its taste was like wheat flour with honey"* (Ex 16:31).

King David, quoting Moses' phrase *"honey from the rock"* (Dt 32:13), gives another eucharistic expression:

> *For I am the Lord your God, who led you out of the land of Egypt. Widen your mouth, and I will fill it... And he fed them from the fat of the grain, and he saturated them with honey from the rock.* (Ps 80:11-17)

The rock is Christ (cf. 1 Cor 10:4); honey is wisdom tasted in consuming Him. If all this were not so, why would the Scriptures connect honey with eternal salvation?

> *eat honey, because it is good, and the honeycomb, because it is so sweet to your throat. So, too, is the doctrine of wisdom to your soul. When you have found it, you will have hope in the end, and your hope shall not perish.* (Prov 24:13-14)

As Holy Communion is sacramental union with God, more generally wisdom is the best of the seven Gifts of the Holy Spirit,

---

[123] *"You nourished your people with the food of angels, and, having prepared bread from heaven, you served them without labor that which holds within itself every delight and the sweetness of every flavour"* (Wis 16:20). After chanting the *Tantum ergo* while adoring the Blessed Sacrament of the Altar, we sing: *"Panem de caelo praestitisti eis. Omne delectamentum in se habentem."* — "Thou hast given them bread from heaven. Having within it all sweetness."

a "connaturality for Divine things [as] the result of charity, which unites us to God".[124]

This interpretation is supported by the story of Samson. His actions were an inspiration of the Holy Spirit (Jdg 14:4,6,19). He proposed a mystery which could not possibly be solved unless explained by its author. As long as Samson kept silent, as the story emphasises three times, nobody could answer his riddle rightly (Jdg 14:6,9,16). So none could have begun to guess at God's Plan with Holy Communion until He spoke of it at the Last Supper. With his enemies moved to murderous frustration, fearing to lose what they had (Jdg 14:13-15; cf. Jn 11:48), Samson like Jesus was betrayed by one close to him (Jdg 14:17,20). Samson's life is far closer to Jesus' than we might first think.

But rather than taking Samson's wife to represent Judas, there is a happier interpretation. The Church Fathers frequently interpret the marriage of a Hebrew to a foreigner as Jesus uniting Himself to the Gentiles. That Samson's father and mother are reluctant to support him in wedding a daughter of the Philistines (Jdg 14:3) speaks of the reluctance of Jews of the synagogue and initially the Church to mix with the heathen (Acts 11:1-3,19; 13:46; 18:6; 21:28). But Samson is determined to marry her, as God is determined to bring 'foreigners' into His fold.

When his wife begs Samson to know the secret of his riddle, *"he explained it. And immediately she revealed it to her countrymen"* (Jdg 14:17). Likewise the Church brings Jesus' Gospel to *"as a light to the revelation of the Gentiles"* (Lk 2:32). The reward for answering the riddle correctly is being awarded linen undergarments and festal tunics (Jdg 14:12-13,19), suitable

---

[124] St Thomas, *S.Th.* II-II, Q.45 a.1.

for a wedding feast, which we can interpret as a cleansed soul dressed over in the glory of God, as such is the proper attire for the Heavenly wedding feast of the Lamb.

At first we might be surprised by the suggestion that the Philistines represent the souls that go to Heaven, since they more usually signify the enemies of God's People; we might be surprised that the woman from Timnah can represent the Church but also Judas; similarly that Samson killing the lion can symbolise the leading judge of Israel killing Jesus, or else in reverse, the Son of God defeating the devil. But typology can work as well by contrast as it can by correspondence. It forms a conceptual chiasma, and there cannot be too much of the Cross! More importantly, it reminds us that God can bring benefit from both good as well as from evil.

Answering the second part of the riddle, the Philistines ask, *"What is stronger than a lion?"* (Jdg 14:17) Well, Jesus. In Him fortitude reaches its zenith, even redemption, as He alone is stronger than death.[125]

What comes from the side of the dead lion then is honey. What comes from the side of Jesus after He expires on the Cross is wisdom. That is, to know how much God loves us, enough to give us His only-begotten Son on Calvary, to give us Him whole and entire in Holy Communion, a love which is more powerful than a lion, invincible.[126]

---

[125] St Bernard of Clairvaux, *Commentary on the Canticle of Canticles,* Sermon XXII.

[126] *"But we preach Christ crucified... the power of God, and the wisdom of God"* (1 Cor 1:23-24 DRB).

This Plan of God's existed long before Samson, and will remain forever: *"The counsel of the Lord remains for eternity, the thoughts of his heart from generation to generation"* (Ps 32:11).

GRACE

The Lord God *turned me back to the gate of the house. And behold, waters went out, from under the threshold of the house, toward the east. For the face of the house looked toward the east. But the waters descended on the right side of the temple, toward the south of the altar... And behold, the waters overflowed on the right side. Then the man who held the rope in his hand departed toward the east, and he measured one thousand cubits. And he led me forward, through the water, up to the ankles. And again he measured one thousand, and he led me forward, through the water, up to the knees. And he measured one thousand, and he led me forward, through the water, up to the waist. And he measured one thousand, into a torrent, through which I was not able to pass. For the waters had risen to become a profound torrent, which was not able to be crossed. And he said to me: 'Son of man, certainly you have seen.' ... And he said to me: 'These waters, which go forth toward the hillocks of sand to the east, and which descend to the plains of the desert, will enter the sea, and will go out, and the waters will be healed. And every living soul that moves, wherever the torrent arrives, will live. And there will be more than enough fish, after these waters have arrived there, and they will be healed. And all things will live, where the torrent arrives. And fishermen will stand over these waters. There will be the drying of nets, from Engedi even to Eneglaim. There will be very many kinds of fish within it: a very great multitude, like the fish of the great sea. But on its shore and in the marshes, they will not be healed. For these will be made into salt pits. And above the torrent, on its banks on both sides, every kind of fruit tree will rise up. Their foliage will not fall away, and their fruit will not fail. Every single month they will bring forth first-fruits. For its waters will go forth from the sanctuary. And its fruits will be for food, and its leaves will be for medicine.'*

— Ezek 47:1-12

In his great vision of the Temple, the prophet Ezekiel saw the life-giving waters flowing from its east gate. In this water was life, such that *"all things shall live to which the torrent shall come"* while outside of it all would die in *"salt pits"* (Ezek 47:9-11). This is the water of saving grace that flows from Christ's side, Christ the true Temple. Even this vision has an earlier foreshadowing in the rock which gushed forth water in the desert for the life of God's People (Ex 17:6).

Ezekiel stresses a detail in his vision, *"behold, the waters overflowed on the right side"* (Ezek 47:2), as tradition has always portrayed the wound of the piercing of Jesus' Heart as on His right side.[127] The further one follows the river, the deeper it becomes, reaching to the ankles, then the knees, then the waist, then *"the waters had risen to become a profound torrent, which was not able to be crossed"* (Ezek 47:5). So is the life of discipleship, grace rising in the individual soul the longer we

---

[127] In Ezek 47:1 the Hebrew reads *"from under the right side of the temple"* using a term for *"side"* (כָּתֵף) which elsewhere is used for the *"shoulder"* of the high priest wearing the Ephod and also for Samson carrying the gates of Gaza, both imagery of Jesus on the Cross (Ex 28:25; Jdg 16:3).

follow Christ until He is entirely dominant; and also the life of the Church as a whole, filling history.

Interestingly, while a question is posited in the Hebrew — *"Son of man, have you seen this?"* (Ezek 47:6 RSVCE); this is rendered in the Latin as an affirmative statement — *"Son of man, certainly you have seen."*[128] Rather than regard this as a conflict in translation, we may receive it as a playful development of the Holy Spirit.[129] We can take the Hebrew text as being before the Crucifixion, and the Latin text as after the Crucifixion. So before the Crucifixion happens the Lord God says, *"Son of man, have you seen this?"* but afterwards, *"Son of man, certainly you have seen."* Today if we claim we do not know what happened on Calvary, then we may be held accountable for wilful blindness.

The growing river flows into the sea, that is into the great eternity (Ezek 47:9). Until the Crucifixion, departed souls were not properly alive. But the waters of the uninhabitable Dead Sea *"will be healed"*; and the waters themselves will heal, so *"all things will live, where the torrent arrives"* (Ezek 47:9).[130] This is sanctifying grace, which poured from the Cross. Now it is received first in Baptism, and increases with every act of charity. If it springs up in our hearts and overflows then it will carry us into the sea of eternal life.

Like other natural things, water is ambivalent in its signification of the supernatural. Dramatically, it represents both death and life: death in the desert, in flash floods, or drowning in

---

[128] Vulgate *"Certe vidisti, fili hominis"*, retained also by the Neo-Vulgate.

[129] Technically this difference may have come about because some texts of the Septuagint have "εἰ ἑώρακας" (a question), whereas in the Codex Vaticanus the "εἰ" is not present, rendering the sentence a statement.

[130] *"from Engedi even to Eneglaim"* (Ezek 47:10) indicates the Dead Sea.

the sea, going under without leaving a trace; but the sea is also where life began (Gen 1:20-21), and water sustains life on earth (Lev 26:4; 1 Kngs 18:1; Ps 146:8; Zech 10:1).[131] So the Easter Vigil ceremonies emphasise that water, *bzw.* Baptism, is indeed both death and life: by it we die with Christ but immediately rise with Him in new life (Rom 6:3-8). Fittingly, Tertullian calls water a most gladsome element.[132]

At some point we will be fished out of this torrent of life. *"Fishermen will stand over these waters"* appointed by Christ for the *"very many kinds of fish within"* (Ezek 47:10; cf. Mt 4:19; 13:47-48). These are both Apostles and angels commissioned to gather in souls.

On both banks will rise up many kinds of trees, *"every kind of fruit tree"* whose *"foliage will not fall away, and their fruit will not fail"* (Ezek 47:7,12). That is, souls who have carried their crosses, who have borne fruit, will harvest the eternal reward for

---

[131] *"[E]very living soul that moves, wherever the torrent arrives, will live"* (Ezek 47:9) echoes creation: *"everything with a living soul and the ability to move that the waters produced"* (Gen 1:21). Translated into the supernatural sphere, we can interpret this to mean that those who have died in friendship with God will be re-vivified by grace for Eternity. Thus *"And He said to me: 'It is done. I am the Alpha and the Omega, the Beginning and the End. To those who thirst, I will give freely from the fountain of the water of life. Whoever prevails shall possess these things. And I will be his God, and he shall be My son. But the fearful, and the unbelieving, and the abominable, and murderers, and fornicators, and drug abusers, and idolaters, and all liars, these shall be a part of the pool burning with fire and sulphur, which is the second death'"* (Apoc 21:6-8; cf. Ezek 47:11).

[132] Tertullian, *De baptismo,* 3 "For the darkness was total thus far, shapeless, without the ornament of stars; and the abyss gloomy; and the earth unfurnished; and the heaven unwrought: water alone — always a perfect, gladsome, simple material substance, pure in itself — supplied a worthy vehicle to God."

the benefit of all. *"Every single month"* means there will be no change, no seasons, no winter in Heaven. In St John's related vision, all fruitfulness is united in Christ:

> *He showed me the river of the water of life, shining like crystal, proceeding from the throne of God and of the Lamb. In the midst of its main street, and on both sides of the river, was the Tree of Life, bearing twelve fruits, offering one fruit for each month, and the leaves of the tree are for the health of the nations.* (Apoc 22:1-2)

The waters of life which enable our entry into Heaven are inseparable from the sanctifying Blood which flows with it, made visible pouring from Christ's side: *"And so, brothers, have faith in the entrance into the Holy of Holies by the Blood of Christ"* (Heb 10:19).

Woe to those who do not die in God's friendship, who pass into the next world without sanctifying grace, untouched by the river of life: *"But on its shore and in the marshes, they will not be healed. For these will be made into salt pits"* (Ezek 47:11). This is the shore where Sodom and Gomorrah were turned to sulphurous sterility. This is hell.

If we refuse the grace which flows from Jesus' Sacred Heart, we will die. If we desire it, if we ask for it, we will live. How shall God convince us of all this? By hiding it throughout the OT, and revealing it with the New. Although the harmony of the Testaments is not the basis of our Faith, it serves a marvellous strengthening of it, inflaming love.

The absolute necessity of receiving God's grace may be grasped if we understand that sanctifying grace is not an assistance to life or condition for life, rather it is life. It is higher than biological life for it is God's life given to us. If we are possessed of this in the moment of our death, then though we die, we will live forever. It is free. Jesus let His Heart be opened to show us that He holds back not one drop of His Life from us.

If we believe, we will see.

III: The Inexhaustible Word

I sleep, yet my heart watches

— Cant 5:3

W hat is God communicating to us through all these prefigurations of Jesus' Passion? First, that the Cross is central to human history. And second, that the Cross is central to our own individual lives, vital for our salvation. If we take the time to meditate upon His Word and see that this is so, then reality is transformed for us: dark into light, bitter into sweet, uncertainty into invincible confidence.

To the first point, the details in a given prefiguration may be fascinating, and surely important in demonstrating God's meticulous concentration on the humblest realities. The variations between the prefigurations make them a delight to discover and ponder. But it is the message of the emergent whole which is most crucial. The bare fact that the Cross has been announced through events in each millennium of human existence prior to the

Crucifixion, coupled with the fact that these events have been recorded and preserved for us in a unique Book, the Bible, so that everyone can be aware of them, ought to convince us that Jesus Christ is the most important Person in history. No one else has the treatment He receives, being heralded in detail from the beginning until His advent. What was most often announced about Him was His Death, yet invariably with His Resurrection, that in Him life comes from death.

This God wants to communicate! Mighty empires came and went to serve God's purpose with Israel, and Israel came and went to serve God's purpose with Christ. Now Israel is returned, doubtless (somehow) to herald Christ again. For as Jesus' Passion had been anticipated through all history before it happened, so it has never been forgotten since, but is remembered daily by millions of souls, especially in the Memorial Jesus made for it, Holy Mass. Therefore we can truly say that the Cross stands at the centre of history. Not, that is, as a mathematical median, but as the goal of history prior to it, the source of history after, and also the ultimate goal, the Crucifixion itself being a prefiguration of what will come to the Church.

> *The things that were first, behold, they have arrived. And I also announce what is new. Before these things arise, I will cause you to hear about them.* (Is 42:9)

Inevitably we are involved in this.

Even if we have made no overarching study to perceive that the Cross stands at the centre of world events, it may well be that we have perceived the truth of the Cross in our own experiences. What we once thought was a personal disaster turns out to be an ineffable blessing. Trials which were dark and almost unbearable to endure are seen later as having been the most rewarding episodes of our lives.

If we have puzzled over the meaning of existence, if we have wondered what the world is coming to, and if our own efforts at understanding simply fail — plus those of all the philosophers and leaders we have consulted or followed — then we are primed to commiserate with St John when he caught sight of the Book of Life in a vision: *"No one was able, neither in heaven, nor on earth, nor under the earth, to open the book, nor to gaze upon it"* (Apoc 5:3). He wept greatly, *"because no one was found worthy to open the book, nor to see it"* (Apoc 5:4).

But one of the elders then said: *"Weep not. Behold, the lion from the tribe of Judah, the root of David, has prevailed to open the book and to break its seven seals"* (Apoc 5:5). St John then saw in the midst of the throne *"a Lamb was standing, as if it were slain"* (Apoc 5:6), who went on to open the Book (Apoc 6:1). The Lamb is evidently Jesus Christ, slain and yet standing, killed and yet resurrected. He is the *"lion of Judah"* and the *"root of David"*, OT allusions to Christ in addition to the Lamb. Jesus Christ crucified, and nobody else, makes sense of the whole Bible, all history and likewise of each human life. Again, God desires to communicate this to us so that we are not left in darkness.

The word for the Lamb 'opening' the Book (ἀνοίγω), and Jesus 'opening' the minds of His Apostles in regard to the OT Scriptures (Lk 24:44-45), is the same for the 'opening' of His Sacred Heart on the Cross (Jn 19:34). Truly in Him are all mysteries contained and revealed. Jesus' Sacred Heart, His love, is our source of life as members of His only beloved Church (as Eve from Adam); as saints (saved as animals from the ark); born and matured in the Sacred Humanity of Christ (by the Sacraments); to know God intimately (which is Wisdom); in the sea of eternity (carried there by the river of life).

The truths of the Cross transform our perception of reality. Is death to be feared? How can we fear it when there awaits on the other side an awakening infinitely more joyful than Adam's when he first laid eyes on Eve? Is life senseless? Take heart from Noah, through whom God arranged the course of nations, even as he lay naked and dead drunk. Shall darkness be a matter for dread, or our intellectual ignorance, when Abraham attests that the undying fire and light are found within it? What of non-Catholics? Abimelech followed the natural law and for that God redeemed him from death. A rock in the desert which Jacob used as a pillow turns out to be the gateway to Heaven: so should we understand every consecrated altar when we come before it, there to 'dream' of the Cross. That place where we all but lost our life (ask Isaac) is the same place as sweet love and the promise of new life.

This whole work is not too hard for us, for Ruth, that is Mary, comes to our aid in every necessity. Even if the whole tide of battle turns against us, the war cannot be lost, for Moses, that is Christ, is watching over the whole theatre and upholding all, while Joshua, our general, that is Christ, is fighting invincibly among us. When the wicked capture and enslave their victims, torture them and scoff in celebration, know that Samson, that is Christ crucified, will bring their temple down on their heads. Even if you sink into what seems like hell, believe Jonah, that God wills to raise you once again to dry land, and that His purpose in you will not fail. Do we see other men as our enemies? We may persecute them like Saul, and die, or have mercy on them like David, and be crowned.

Would anyone say reverence for the Holy Eucharist is a small matter, when Joseph, that is Christ, revealed to the butler and baker that it is life and death? If witnessing to Christ provokes the ferocity of the world against us, does that mean we have made a mistake? God showed Elijah it was not so, even giving him supernatural food to continue. Life cannot be grasped on our terms, but only received on God's, such is the miserable lesson from Lot's daughters. Time will run out, God's patience will end. Ezekiel has shown us.

There remain many sleeps to be explored. Though we might grow tired, truly the Word of God is inexhaustible.

Samuel needed three sleeps before he understood God's message, illustrating that divine revelation is multi-staged, coming to us in the book of nature, then through the Torah and finally in the Logos assuming Flesh (1 Sam 3).

Daniel was seized by revelatory visions, falling *"into a deep sleep with my face to the ground"* (Dan 8:18; 10:9 RSVCE), the same *"sleep"* in Hebrew (רְדַּם) as Jonah (Jon 1:5-6), who then faced three days in the watery tomb.

Another prophet, Jeremiah, after announcing the incarnation, speaks of awaking from sweet sleep to introduce the new Covenant (Jer 31:22,26,31*ff*). He was personally put into the filthy pit (like Hades) by the leaders of Jerusalem, spending days there in darkness, but finally resurrected (Jer 38:1-13). The same king, signifying God, who permitted him to be sunk also ordered him to be rescued.

Jacob's wife Leah, older and blear-eyed in contrast to her beautiful younger sister Rachel, played a trick which backfired. By her own scheming, Leah's sleep with Jacob was less fruitful than Rachel's, so the blessing of the father went from the elder to the younger. In like manner the Temple gave way to the Church (Gen 30:16).

Skipping over Jacob's vision of the ladder, in another dream he is assured of the inevitable fruitfulness and security of the Holy Spirit (Gen 31:11-14). Later, in a revival of spirit *"as if from a deep sleep"* or stunned numbness and shock, we see in Jacob's waking the shared life of Father and Son (Gen 45:26), as *"his life is bound up in the lad's life"* (Gen 44:30).[133] Jacob's final sleep promises resurrection with the saints (Gen 47:30).

"I sleep, yet my heart watches," sings the Bride (Cant 5:1-3), indicating *"love is strong as death, jealousy as hard as hell"* (Cant 8:6), for even in Jesus' death His Heart watches, rescuing His future Bride, His divine jealousy a rage overcoming His rival.

In contrast to this Solomon observes that a worldly, distracted life, one without sleep, is empty (Eccl 8:16), like one who flees the Cross.

If after so many sleeps, one is convinced that the Passion of Christ is prefigured through the OT, then further types for the Sacrifice of Calvary are found to abound. Jesus Himself said:

> *And just as Moses lifted up the serpent in the desert, so also must the Son of man be lifted up, so that whoever believes in Him may not perish, but may have eternal life.* (Jn 3:14-15)

Therefore Moses holding up the bronze serpent in the desert is infallibly a prefiguration of Calvary. Those who faced death from the fiery serpents needed only to look upon the serpent's image held up by Moses to be saved (Num 21:4-9). How can this signify the Cross? Because it is sin which stings us and brings us death,

---

133 Vulgate:. *"Quo audito Jacob, quasi de gravi somno evigilans... revixit spiritus ejus"* (Gen 45:26-27).

and if we raise our eyes to Christ on the Cross there are two things we may see there. The eyes of the body see agony, Blood and death — and we must confess that it is our sins that nailed Jesus there, our sins that crucified Him. Yet the eyes of the mind perceive self-sacrifice and the mildest of mercy, and the heart knows love and redemption. The Cross is darkness and light simultaneously. So while Jesus carried our sins in His Body, it was sin which was defeated on the Cross: Jesus rose; the serpent was crucified forever. This we should see on Calvary as well as in the image Moses made of it beforehand and in the memorial Jesus bequeathed of it forever — Holy Mass.

Jonathan prefigured the Crucifixion by gorging on honey. We remember honey signifies wisdom, yet we can only take it in measure.[134] Jonathan was so replete with it that his eyes and his whole face shone. The brief account contains in five verses the themes of father and son, of kingship, of a sign for the removal of iniquity from Israel, of lots cast, of the son condemned for being filled with wisdom (honey), his taking the wood in his hand and his being willing to die, and yet escaping from death, to the great joy of the people (1 Sam 14:41-45).

David went into hiding for two or three days in the field, as Jesus in the tomb, after a death sentence from Saul, that is the authorities. But Jonathan, son of the king, comes to communicate with his dear David in a manner mysterious which none but they understand. And *"David rose up from his place"* (1 Sam 20:41). David and Jonathan are united like the Humanity and Divinity of Christ: *"May the Lord be between me and you, and between my offspring and your offspring, even forever"*.

---

[134] *"Thou hast found honey, eat what is sufficient for thee, lest being glutted therewith thou vomit it up"* (Prov 25:16 DRB).

203

Later David slept chastely with a beautiful virgin before finally he closed his eyes the last time (1 Kngs 1:4). So Christ's last sleep meant His spiritual union with His Bride, the Church.[135]

Absalom, son of David, rode on a mule, hung from a tree and was pierced with a spear, with the result that countless Israeli lives were spared (2 Sam 18:8-17). How did such a soldier make such an error, to ride into a tree? Perhaps he did not see it, perhaps weary from battle his eyes were closed? Perhaps he was sleeping. It would fit with the pattern above.

The plenitude of pain expressed in David's repetitious mourning for Absalom shows the Father not indifferent to His Son (albeit impassible in Heaven):

בְּנִי אַבְשָׁלוֹם בְּנִי בְנִי אַבְשָׁלוֹם מִי־יִתֵּן
מוּתִי אֲנִי תַחְתֶּיךָ אַבְשָׁלוֹם בְּנִי בְנִי :

υἱέ μου Αβεσσαλωμ, υἱέ μου υἱέ μου Αβεσσαλωμ, τίς δῴη τὸν θάνατόν μου ἀντὶ σοῦ, ἐγὼ ἀντὶ σοῦ; Αβεσσαλωμ υἱέ μου υἱέ μου

Fili mi Absalom, Absalom fili mi: quis mihi tribuat ut ego moriar pro te, Absalom fili mi, fili mi Absalom?

My son Absalom! Absalom my son! Who can grant to me that I may die on your behalf? Absalom, my son! My son, Absalom!

(2 Sam 18:33)

---

[135] David fought Goliath without armour, like Christ dying on the Cross naked, or else in His defeating satan in His human nature, not using divine power to do it, for satan lost on Good Friday. The five smooth stones David carried speak of the five wounds of Christ on the Cross: one of them was enough. Any drop of His Blood could redeem the cosmos.

In the examples given so far, most involve a person prefiguring Christ. But there are also all those Paschal lambs, the scapegoats, the bulls, sheep and daily lambs and doves. Or if one were to try to enumerate all the mentions in Sacred Scripture where wood prefigures the Cross, or bread and wine the Holy Eucharist, or blood and altars the scene on Calvary, or the High Priest and Sanctuary the mystical purpose, there would literally be hundreds of examples.

There are so many words in the Bible which anticipate the Crucifixion that if the explorations and meditations on *"each of these were written down, the world itself, I suppose, would not be able to contain the books that would be written"* (Jn 21:25).

Indeed the whole world ceaselessly declares the same truths. To see any tree or piece of wood, to glance at any drop of wine or loaf of bread, any grape or grain or fruit or seed, is to be reminded of God's Plan for our redemption through the Crucifixion. Our Saviour taught:

> *Amen, amen, I say to you, unless the grain of wheat falls to the ground and dies, it remains alone. But if it dies, it yields much fruit. Whoever loves his life, will lose it. And whoever hates his life in this world, preserves it unto eternal life.* (Jn 12:24-25)

Every grain of wheat preaches Christ's Sacrifice of Calvary. So does every sleep. The whole land sleeps in winter so it can awake with spring. The moon's wanes into darkness so it can wax again bright. The sun sets so it may rise. Annually, monthly, daily, we are invited to experience the central truth of creation. God made sleep to teach us of the Passion, to show us not to fear death, to confirm our belief in the resurrection.

If everywhere nature declares the Gospel, how much more every page of the OT. God wrote both. The world accounts this madness. But the folly of God is wiser than the wisdom of this world (1 Cor 1:25).

> *I stand unto this day, witnessing both to small and great, saying no other thing than those which the prophets, and Moses did say should come to pass: That Christ should suffer, and that He should be the first that should rise from the dead, and should shew light to the people, and to the Gentiles. As he spoke these things... Festus said with a loud voice: 'Paul, thou art beside thyself: much learning doth make thee mad.' And Paul said: 'I am not mad, most excellent Festus, but I speak words of truth and soberness.'* (Acts 26:22-25 DRB)

Apparent madness turns out to be truth. The goodness of the Cross is so contrary to appearances, the good operation of the Cross so unexpected, that our hearts must be reduced of all self-sufficiency to accept it. When Jesus told His Apostles of His Passion in advance, they were not enthused (Mt 17:21-23). They could not grasp it (Mt 20:18-28; Lk 18:31-34). They even rebuked Him (Mk 8:31-33; 9:30-31). When it finally came they fled (Mt 26:56); it seemed senseless to stay. Afterwards, on Pentecost, the Apostles preached the truth of the Cross to the world gathered in Jerusalem, and were deemed drunk (Acts 2:13).

Of primary interest here is not the world's lack of understanding before, during and after the Crucifixion, but that in the Gospels we read of the Crucifixion first before it happened (Mt 2:16,18; 26:2,24,28,45); then its operation revealed while it was happening (Lk 23:43,46; Jn 19:26-27; 19:30); and then it being recalled by the Evangelists afterward (Mt 28:5-7; Mk 16:6; Lk 24:6-8,25-27,44-48; Jn 20:9,27-29). This is a marvellous snapshot of all reality. Calvary was announced from the beginning of history and will be remembered to the end — because it is the central event, the most important. Jesus was prefigured in the murdered prophets (Mt 23:29-37; Lk 6:22-23) and then imitated after in murdered martyrs (Jn 15:20; Acts 7:52,55-59; 12:2). These are the lives that shape history most profoundly because they are closest to the Cross.

Another way to take all of this in is to consider the problem of the one and the many. Some ancient philosophers argued that all being is one. Opposing this, others taught that reality is an irreducible multitude, that being is necessarily many. Aristotle gave a solution so elegant it shines with truth: transcendent Being is One, and it is through participation in the One that being is enjoyed by the many, each in their multifarious ways. Applying this solution in the light of revelation, we say God alone is Self-Subsistent Being, but through His Son, the Word, ὁ Λογος, innumerable creatures come into existence. Highest among all these creatures are persons, countless of whom come to eternal life with God through Jesus Christ, by way of His Death and Resurrection. Jesus' Passion is the key to reality because it provides the highest solution to the problem of the one and the many. His saints participate in Him. They live in Him because He lives in them.

We may be impressed to see how Christ influenced the lives of St Stephen, or St Theresa of Avila, or St Thomas More. But there is a danger we misunderstand, thinking this is merely extrinsic, as if the main agent were the particular saint. Prefigurations defuse this misunderstanding because once we see that Jesus' Passion really was the cause of the histories of Jonah, and Abraham, and Noah, and Adam, then immediately we confess these are divine workings of God Who alone can transcend all time. If we admit two or three prefigurations, we might still claim it is coincidence. But when we see a dozen, or a score, or finally lose count, there is no room left for doubt that God Himself planted the Cross to reach all His children.

A further difference between the saints before Christ and those after Him is to emphasise God's work in our salvation and our cooperation respectively. All the saints since Christ shine with holiness, with moral goodness; there is no doubt that they strained their wills to conform themselves to Christ. Always their salvation is first a gift of God, but they make clear that we are meant to merit it too. The OT prefigurations on the other hand emphasise not our efforts but God's election. It is true that some of them were moral beacons; Joseph, Moses and Elijah come to mind. But their showing forth the Cross in the cases studied above was much more a matter of election than merit. The point is clearer still with Jacob, Samson and Jonah. I have no doubt they were each exceedingly holy, but that is not immediately conveyed by the Scriptures. Rather the Bible shows God chose to act through them and that is why we know them at all. Adam and Boaz, in their prefigurations at least, did little more noble than fall asleep. And yet who can deny their greatness in Christ? It is good for us to be reminded that closeness to God is first of all a matter of His election, and secondarily of our wholehearted response.

When we glimpse how Christ gives eternal sense to the lives of OT figures, persons whose lives had previously been, to put it gently, a puzzle to us, then this reverberates to the glory of God. We see how their many lives are elevated, which in turn abounds to the glory of God. And as our esteem for Christ increases, then the light He throws out becomes brighter, making sense — in our understanding — of even more lives than before. There is a resonance from glory unto glory. Typology (wherein figures from the past are fulfilled in what comes later) does not demean type or archetype, but elevates both, conserving the distinct identity of persons, but manifesting an ever greater unity the more members it draws into a more perfectly perceived One.[136]

Or how else shall we know God except through the Son, through Jesus Christ? And how shall we increase in knowledge of Him without increasing in knowledge of His saints? The more we know of the more of them, and love what we know, the better we know and love Christ.

This is the process by which we get to know anything high. Aristotle said it was difficult to define the soul, for one was not sure whether to start by defining the essence and then study her attributes, or start with her attributes in order to discern her essence.[137] The difficulty is that, being invisible, we cannot simply 'start with the essence' of the soul, because we do not at first know what she is. Yet it is also difficult to start with the attributes, because if we do not know what she is, how do we know which attributes belong to the soul and which do not? Aristotle's answer was to shuttle between the two. One notices certain attributes and ventures a primitive definition. From here one can test more attributes, which should help in refining the definition. Finally one hopes to come up with a precise answer. In *De anima:* "The soul is the first actuality of a natural body that has life potentially".

---

[136] See Paolo Prosperi, *Toward a Renewal of Typological Exegesis* in *Communio 37* (Fall 2010), p.389*ss*.

[137] Aristotle, *De anima*, I.

If that definition is obscure to us, so is Jesus Christ when we first hear of Him. But by going from Him to His best works, that is His saints, and returning from them to Him, we enter a reverberation whereby Christ is apprehended as drawing in literally all who are saved, who respond to Him, who love (Prov 14:31; 19:17; Mt 25:31-46; Jn 15:12).

Every act of love in the whole history of the planet finds its source and end in Jesus Christ. He is the most significant answer to the problem of the one and the many. Jesus is the One, we are the many. We go back to the One, but this time with billions of participants in Him. Their lives are raised by His, they are covered in His glory. And He rises thereby higher in our understanding, higher than we ever imagined before. Prefigurations have a special role because of their undeniably divine character. The accumulation of such cases attests that truly His Sacrifice stands in the centre of each human life.

Finding the Passion of Christ in the OT corroborates our faith and gives us inspiration in our trials. It serves our salvation and gives glory to God. The darkest event to have ever occurred on this planet is, in fact, the most blessed.

ABOUT THE AUTHOR

Born in 1973, James Mawdsley grew up in Lancashire, England. He is author of *The Heart Must Break: The Fight for Democracy and Truth in Burma* (Century, 2001), detailing his three detentions as a political prisoner in Burma. During seventeen months of solitary confinement he received the Bible which helped turn his cell from "hell to heaven", and without which, this current book would doubtless not be written.

From 2003 to 2004, having met former prisoners and guards who had defected from North Korea, Mawdsley served as the first Secretariat to the British-North Korean All-Party Parliamentary Group, sitting in on high-level political-military meetings in Pyongyang and London. His priority in arranging these exchanges was to challenge the North Korean government for their gulag system.

Slowly realising the futility of political attempts to overcome evil unless Jesus Christ is honoured as King of Kings, Mawdsley was surprised on 3rd September 2005 by a crystal-clear call to the priesthood. He was ordained a Catholic priest in 2016 for the traditional Roman rite.

THE NEW OLD SERIES

- *Adam's Deep Sleep: The Passion of Jesus Christ Prefigured in the Old Testament* (2022)

- *Crushing satan's head: The Virgin Mary's Victory over the Antichrist Foretold in the Old Testament* (2022)

- *Crucifixion to Creation: Roots of the Traditional Mass Traced back to Paradise* (2023)

Made in United States
Orlando, FL
03 December 2022

25429257R00120